D1093515

THE NEW TEMPLE SHAKESPEARE

Edited by M. R. Ridley, M.A.

THE TEMPEST

by William Shakespeare

London: J. M. DENT & SONS LTD.
New York: E. P. DUTTON & CO. INC.

Editor's General Note

The Text. The editor has kept before him the aim of presenting to the modern reader the nearest possible approximation to what Shakespeare actually wrote. The text is therefore conservative, and is based on the earliest reliable printed text. But to avoid distraction (*a*) the spelling is modernised, and (*b*) a limited number of universally accepted emendations is admitted without comment. Where a Quarto text exists as well as the First Folio the passages which occur only in the Quarto are enclosed in square brackets [ ] and those which occur only in the Folio in brace brackets { }.

Scene Division. The rapid continuity of the Elizabethan curtainless production is lost by the 'traditional' scene divisions. Where there is an essential difference of place these scene divisions are retained. Where on the other hand the change of place is insignificant the scene division is indicated only by a space on the page. For ease of reference, however, the 'traditional' division is retained at the head of the page and in line numbering.

Notes. Passages on which there are notes are indicated by a † in the margin.

Punctuation adheres more closely than has been usual to the 'Elizabethan' punctuation of the early texts. It is often therefore more indicative of the way in which the lines were to be delivered than of their syntactical construction.

Glossaries are arranged on a somewhat novel principle, not alphabetically, but in the order in which the words or phrases occur. The editor is much indebted to Mr J. N. Bryson for his collaboration in the preparation of the glossaries.

Preface

The Text. The play appeared in print for the first time (so far as we know) in the First Folio. The text is on the whole good. There is a certain amount of mislineation, but comparatively few obvious typographical errors. There are some obscure passages, a few of which are obviously corrupt, while more may be either Shakespeare's fault, or the compositor's, or both. The punctuation is both careful and interesting, though I see no need to rhapsodise about it. The stage-directions are unusually elaborate and complete; the New Cambridge editors say that they 'bear the unmistakable impress of the master's hand'; but since we have no external criterion for determining which stage-directions of other plays in the Folio are Shakespeare's, which the prompter's, and which perhaps the insertions of someone editing copy for the Folio edition, any editor who is prepared to find on a particular set of stage-directions 'the unmistakable impress of the master's hand' (which means, I take it, that they were certainly written by Shakespeare) is being certainly very courageous and perhaps unwise. Their very elaboration rather suggests a manuscript prepared for a reader, and does not, I think, suit too well with the other conclusion of the same editors that the copy for *The Tempest* was very probably the author's MS. which had served as theatre prompt-copy. The stage-directions in texts which there is reason to suppose were printed from prompt-copy have a way of being laconic imperatives, like *Sound Horns*. The text here given is that of the First Folio with the minimum of alteration. Whether that text is the play as Shakespeare wrote it, or the result of revision or of cutting or of both, need not perhaps exercise us very seriously, since in any event the Folio text is all the text we have. But one or two of the problems are discussed in the next section.

Date of Composition. There is no doubt that the play, presumably in the shape in which we have it, was one of the ' fourteen severall playes ' presented at court by John Heminge in the winter of 1612-13 as part of the celebrations for the betrothal and wedding of King James's daughter, the Princess Elizabeth, to the Prince Palatine Elector. There is also little doubt that it was presented at Court in some shape in November 1611. The New Cambridge editors have an elaborate theory of revision and abridgment, which would put the final revision in 1612 and the first draft of the play as much earlier in Shakespeare's dramatic career as we choose. Since *The Tempest* was the first play published in the New Cambridge edition, and since in it the textual editor clearly explained and strikingly exemplified his methods of attack on textual problems, it will perhaps not be impertinent here to examine briefly these methods in action on the problem in front of us. I have commented on some of the theories of the New Cambridge editors in the prefaces to other plays in this edition, and I hope to say something in more detail of their work as a whole in the companion volume to this edition. The New Cambridge edition is beyond question a notable landmark in the history of Shakespearean scholarship ; for the first time there are being applied to the determination of the text of Shakespeare those new tools which the bibliographical and other researches of the last thirty years have put into the hands of its editors. And no student or editor of Shakespeare can fail to admire the exact knowledge that directs their work and the trained imagination which informs it, nor dare he neglect to examine their conclusions with the greatest care. But I think that one may question whether they are not sometimes betrayed, by delight in their tools, into regarding them as instruments of precision by which exact conclusions can be determined rather than as aids to reasonable and illuminating conjecture, and whether also they are not sometimes tempted, by the pleasure of solution, into finding a problem where no problem is. But it will not, I hope, be supposed, because in the Notes to this play I have allowed myself rather more freedom than usual in criticising some of their detailed points, and in this and other prefaces question some of their more general conclusions, that I am any the less conscious of the importance of their work and of my own debt to it.

In his chapter on the copy for *The Tempest*, the New Cambridge textual editor starts out quite decisively with the statement : " The condition of the Folio text appears to show that the *Tempest* MS. had seen many changes before it reached the printer's hands." The evidence for these changes and the characteristics of them are then summarised under various heads. Attention is first drawn to "traces of rhymed couplets at III. i. 24-5, 29-30, III. iii. 32-3, 49-51, and elsewhere, together with the doggerel at III. ii. 78-80. These are taken to suggest that " when Shakespeare took up the *Tempest* late in his career he had an old MS. to go upon, possibly an early play of his own, which may have been related to the original of *Die Schöne Sidea*, a sixteenth-century German drama with a kindred theme." One may notice that the question is here begged at the outset in the phrase " when Shakespeare took up the *Tempest* late in his career," unless indeed that means no more than ' when Shakespeare began work on *The Tempest*,' since for all that at present we know Shakespeare started *The Tempest* as a new play late in his career. As to the evidence of traces of rhymed couplets, I have elsewhere, *e.g.*, in the Preface to *As You Like It*, and in a note on *Much Ado*, IV. i. 209, shown reason to be suspicious of the evidence of 'fossils,' and I do not think that the supposed couplets here are particularly convincing, nor indeed the doggerel. A quarter of an hour's research in *Othello* produced the following parallels:

> Cas.   *I pray you, sir, go forth,*
>   *And give us truth, who 'tis that is arriv'd.*
> 2 Gent. *I shall*
> Mon.   *But, good lieutenant, is your general wiv'd?*
>
>   (II. i. 57-60)

(where we need only to omit the unnecessary remark of the second gentleman to have an excellent couplet);

> *When you shall these unlucky deeds relate,*
> *Speak of them as they are ; nothing extenuate,*
>
>   (V. ii. 348-9)

which needs only slight amputation;
and here are unmistakable traces of *abcb* quatrains in *Antony and Cleopatra*:

> *It is asham'd to bear me. Friends, come hither,*
> *I am so lated in the world that I*
> *Have lost my way for ever. I have a ship*
> *Laden with gold, take that, divide it ; fly,*
>
>   (III. xi. 2-5)

> *I have myself resolv'd upon a course*
> *Which has no need of you ; be gone,*
> *My treasur's in the harbour, take it. O,*
> *I follow'd that I blush to look upon,*
>
>   (ib. 9-12)

The next statement is that the received text has been clearly
abridged, and abridged in the main by Shakespeare himself, and
the signs of this abridgment are said to be many. In the first
place, *The Tempest* is the shortest text but two in the canon. That
is perfectly true, but unless we suppose that Shakespeare had a
normal length of play, and that he could not, whether for a special
occasion, or merely because he felt like it, write a short play that
was yet as long as he wanted it, the shortness of *The Tempest* is
evidence of nothing at all. " Broken lines abound in it, as do
passages of incorrect verse lining—a sure sign of marginal alteration in a good text." There is no doubt about the presence of
the broken lines and the mislineation, but as to the broken lines
one cannot, I think, have it both ways, and when one finds the
same editor commenting on V. i. 61 that " this broken line is too
effective not to be intentional," we feel that the broken-line evidence
is somewhat weakened. And the statement that mislineation is a
sure sign of marginal alteration in a good text seems to me to be
a statement which goes beyond any available evidence. No doubt
marginal alteration is a probable explanation of otherwise un-
accountable mislineation, but until we have an original MS. with
marginal alteration, and also an Elizabethan text printed from that
copy which exhibits mislineation, we cannot, I think, legitimately
speak of " a sure sign." Further, even if we accept this mislineation as clear evidence of marginal alteration, there is no proof
at all that the marginal alterations might not have been made in
the heat of composition, rather than after a considerable interval
of time. The next points are, I think, stronger evidence that
something happened, namely, " the unsystematic mingling of verse
and prose, *e.g.* in the wreck-scene and the Stephano scenes," and
the respective absence and presence of Antonio's son, who is

mentioned but never appears, and Francisco, who appears only to deliver two non-significant remarks which might just as well have been delivered by somebody else. We then come on to the following: "Perhaps however the clearest indication of all is the immense second scene, which comprises almost a quarter of the whole play. Most of this scene is taken up with an account of events which we may assume provided the material for pre-wreck scenes in the earlier version. *The Tempest* is, indeed, remarkable in having three separate expositions . . . the threefold difficulty is tackled by Shakespeare with consummate skill; but the expositions are there, and they tell their own tale. At some stage of its evolution *The Tempest* was in all likelihood a loosely constructed drama like *A Winter's Tale* and *Pericles*." It will be observed that we have now advanced to "*the* earlier version," as though the hypothesis of such a version's existence had been already proved, in spite of the fact that this second scene is supposed to be part of the proof. And why is there any reason to suppose that at any stage of its evolution—even supposing that it had an evolution of this kind— *The Tempest* was a loosely constructed drama? It is pointed out by all critics, including the New Cambridge editors themselves, that in the "exposition" of *The Tempest* Shakespeare brilliantly solved a dramatic problem. And why should we imagine that he could only solve it by the slow method of writing the play wrong first and then correcting his initial errors?

That the masque was a later insertion we may however take it, I think, as proved. The evidence is somewhat complicated, but convincing. But even complete certainty as to the insertion of the masque would have no relevance at all to a theory of a previous "evolution" of the play; the masque might quite well have been inserted in 1612 into a play which had been written in one stretch of dramatic creation in 1611, though it is suggested that the suggested crudity of the abridgment in the second section of Act I, Scene ii is connected with the insertion of the masque, "which would naturally involve curtailment somewhere else." But as one of the reasons for which we are asked to suppose that the text of *The Tempest* has had a vexed history is the present shortness of the play, there seems no reason why the insertion of the not very long masque should have involved any curtailment at all.

As to the exact state of the text presented to us in the Folio, quite apart from the stages by which the copy for it came to be what it was, the New Cambridge textual editor imagines a compositor who, though he in the main normalised Shakespeare's spelling, was weak on grammar and also suffered from a liability to hypnosis. He is also supposed to have followed with great exactitude Shakespeare's own punctuation, except in a number of places where the Folio punctuation does not commend itself to the editor, and the compositor has therefore been careless.

For reasons indicated earlier in the Preface, a good deal more space than usual is allotted in the Notes at the end of this volume to the discussion of various points connected with the text and the methods of the New Cambridge editors.

Sources. On this subject much has been said, much might be said to little profit, and I propose to say very little. Collins (the poet) is recorded by Thomas Warton as giving a "favourite romance," *Aurelio and Isabella*, as a source; but either Collins got the name of the romance wrong or he had forgotten its contents, since the resemblances are of the slightest. That there is some relation between Shakespeare's play and *Die Schöne Sidea* of Jacob Ayrer of Nuremberg is clear; but which way round the connection is, or whether both plays derived from a common source, is not clear at all, nor at all important. By far the most interesting and certain sources are the various pamphlets describing the adventures of the expedition of nine ships and five hundred colonists which set out in May of 1609 for the new colony of Virginia. The flagship, the *Sea-Adventure*, carrying the leaders of the expedition, Sir Thomas Gates and Sir George Somers, was wrecked on the Bermudas; but all on board were saved, built ships on the island, and reached Virginia in the next year, whence the accounts of their adventures were sent to England. For a full discussion of the various accounts, and their respective importance for the study of *The Tempest*, readers must be referred to the admirable summary in the (recently revised) Arden edition of the play.

Duration of Action. Of this little need be said. It is almost as though Shakespeare, in answer to a challenge, was showing that he could, when he chose, observe the unities as narrowly as he could spaciously violate them. *The Tempest* observes the unity of time by many hours more exactly than the more rigid purists demand. In *The Winter's Tale* the represented time exceeds the stage time by sixteen years; in *The Tempest* the excess is perhaps half an hour.

Criticism. I wish that there was space to quote Coleridge at length, since *The Tempest* stimulated him to a rather unusually sustained excellence of criticism, so that his remarks lend themselves much less readily than usual to selection. I give therefore only the concluding general remarks of the 1811 lecture on *The Tempest*, together with excerpts from Hazlitt and Swinburne.

Coleridge.—If Shakespeare be the wonder of the ignorant, he is, and ought to be, much more the wonder of the learned: not only from profundity of thought, but from his astonishing and intuitive knowledge of what man must be at all times, and under all circumstances, he is rather to be looked upon as a prophet than as a poet. Yet, with all these unbounded powers, with all this might and majesty of genius, he makes us feel as though he were unconscious of himself, and of his high destiny, disguising the half god in the simplicity of a child.

Hazlitt.—*The Tempest* is one of the most original and perfect of Shakespear's productions, and he has shewn in it all the variety of his powers. It is full of grace and grandeur. The human and imaginary characters, the dramatic and the grotesque, are blended together with the greatest art, and without any appearance of it. Though he has here given " to airy nothing a local habitation and a name," yet that part which is only the fantastic creation of his mind, has the same palpable texture, and coheres " semblably " with the rest. As the preternatural part has the air of reality, and almost haunts the imagination with a sense of truth, the real characters and events partake of the wildness of a dream. . . .

The character of Caliban is generally thought (and justly so) to be one of the author's masterpieces. It is not indeed pleasant to see this character on the stage any more than it is to see the God Pan personated there. But in itself it is one of the wildest and most abstracted of all Shakespear's characters, whose deformity whether of body or mind is redeemed by the power and truth of the imagination displayed in it. It is the essence of grossness, but there is not a particle of vulgarity in it. Shakespear has described the brutal mind of Caliban in contact with the pure and original forms of nature; the character grows out of the soil where it is rooted uncontrouled, uncouth and wild, uncramped by any of the meannesses of custom. It is "of the earth, earthy." It seems almost to have been dug out of the ground, with a soul instinctively superadded to it answering to its wants and origin. Vulgarity is not natural coarseness, but conventional coarseness, learnt from others, contrary to, or without an entire conformity of natural power and disposition; as fashion is the common-place affection of what is elegant and refined without any feeling of the essence of it. Schlegel, the admirable German critic on Shakespear, observes that Caliban is a poetical character, and "always speaks in blank verse." . . .

Shakespear has, as it were by design, drawn off from Caliban the elements of whatever is ethereal and refined, to compound them in the unearthly mould of Ariel. Nothing was ever more finely conceived than this contrast between the material and the spiritual, the gross and delicate. Ariel is imaginary power, the swiftness of thought personified. . . .

The courtship between Ferdinand and Miranda is one of the chief beauties of this play. It is the very purity of love. The pretended interference of Prospero with it heightens its interest, and is in character with the magician, whose sense of preternatural power makes him arbitrary, tetchy, and impatient of opposition.

Swinburne.[1]—True or false, and it would now seem something less than likely to be true, the fancy which assumed the last lines spoken by Prospero to be likewise the last words of the last completed work of Shakespeare was equally in either case at once

[1] Reprinted from *A Study of Shakespeare* by permission of the publishers, W Heinemann Ltd.

natural and graceful. There is but one figure sweeter than Miranda's and sublimer than Prospero's in all the range of heaven on which the passion of our eyes could rest at parting. And from one point of view there is even a more heavenly quality perceptible in the light of this than of its two twin stars. In no nook or corner of the island as we leave it is any savour left or any memory lingering of any inexpiable evil. Alonzo is absolved; even Antonio and Sebastian have made no such ineffaceable mark on it by the presence of their pardoned crimes as is made by those which cost the life of Mamillius and the labours of Imogen. Poor Caliban is left in such comfort as may be allowed him by divine grace in the favourable aspect of Setebos; and his comrades go by us " reeling ripe " and " gilded " not by " grand liquor " only but also by the summer lightning of men's laughter: blown softly out of our sight, with a sound and a gust of music, by the breath of the song of Ariel.

The Occasion. I append a section absent from other prefaces in this edition for a particular purpose and a particular pleasure. The purpose is to suggest that our appreciation of this play, in many ways as ' universal ' and timeless a play as any that Shakespeare ever wrote, is movingly enhanced if we remember, as we read, the circumstances of its presentation. The pleasure is that of quoting a piece of criticism which illuminates these circumstances. Whether or not the play was in fact the last that Shakespeare wrote, I am sure that the general instinct of readers has been right, and that in some degree he felt it as his farewell to the theatre, a farewell delivered in 1611. But it was presented again in 1612-13, and it stirs the imagination to remember that it was this particularly personal play of Shakespeare's, almost certainly adapted for the occasion by the insertion of the masque, which was selected for the celebrations of the betrothal of a particular girl of sixteen, and played before her for her delight.

Who that girl was 'Q' may tell us : '. . . the incomparable Queen of Hearts whose name in story is Elizabeth of Bohemia,

design'd
Th' eclipse and glory of her kind.

For " beauty vanishes, beauty passes," but the charm of this woman still fascinates the imagination almost as in her life-time it won and compelled the souls of men to champion her sorrowful fortunes. That it did this—that it laid on the nobler spirits of her time a spell potent to extravagance and yet so finely apportioned as almost to serve us now for a test and gauge of their nobility— no reader of early seventeenth-century biography will deny. The evidence is no less frequent than startling. It would almost seem that no " gentleman " could come within the aura but he knelt to Elizabeth of Bohemia, her sworn knight : that either he followed thenceforth to the last extremity, proud only to serve, or, called away, he departed as one who had looked upon a vision which changed all the values of life, who had beheld a kingdom of the soul in which self and this world were well lost for a dream. We may see this strange conversion in Wotton; we may trace it in the careers of Donne, of Dudley Carleton and (with a postscript of morose disillusion) Lord Herbert of Cherbury. . . . We may see this exuberance carried into steady practice by Lord Craven, a Lord Mayor's son, who having poured blood and money in her service, laid his last wealth at her feet to provide her a stately refuge and a home. Through all the story she—grand-daughter of Mary of Scotland, mother of Rupert of the Rhine—rides reck-

less, feckless, spendthrift, somehow ineffably great; conquering all
hearts near her, that

> *—Enamour'd do wish so they might*
> *But enjoy such a sight,*
> *That they still were to run by her side*
> *Thoro' swords, thoro' seas, whither she would ride.*

lifting all those gallant hearts to ride with her, for a desperate
cause, despising low ends, ignoble gain; to ride with her down
and nobly over the last lost edge of the world.' Before this
woman, then a newly-betrothed girl, bidding a high-spirited farewell to the country to which, fifty years later, after all her sorrowful
adventures she returned to die, Shakespeare's *The Tempest* was
presented.

THE TEMPEST

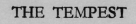

DRAMATIS PERSONÆ

ALONSO, *King of Naples.*

SEBASTIAN, *his brother.*

PROSPERO, *the right Duke of Milan.*

ANTONIO, *his brother, the usurping Duke of Milan.*

FERDINAND, *son to the King of Naples.*

GONZALO, *an honest old Counsellor.*

ADRIAN,
FRANCISCO, } *Lords.*

CALIBAN, *a savage and deformed Slave.*

TRINCULO, *a Jester.*

STEPHANO, *a drunken Butler.*

Master of a Ship.

Boatswain.

Mariners.

MIRANDA, *daughter to Prospero.*

ARIEL, *an airy Spirit.*

IRIS,
CERES,
JUNO, } *presented by Spirits.*
Nymphs,
Reapers,

Other Spirits attending on Prospero.

THE TEMPEST

Act First

SCENE I

On a ship at sea : a tempestuous noise of thunder and lightning heard

Enter a Ship-Master, and a Boatswain

Mas. Boatswain ! †

Bo. Here, master : what cheer ?

Mas. Good ; speak to the mariners : fall to 't, yarely, or we run ourselves aground, bestir, bestir. *Exit*

Enter Mariners

Bo. Heigh, my hearts, cheerly, cheerly, my hearts ! yare, yare ! Take in the topsail. Tend to the master's whistle. Blow till thou burst thy wind, if room † enough !

Enter Alonso, Sebastian, Antonio, Ferdinand, Gonzalo, and others

Al. Good boatswain, have care : where 's the master ? Play the men.   10

Bo. I pray now keep below.

1

Ant. Where is the master, boatswain ?

Bo. Do you not hear him ?   You mar our labour, keep your cabins : you do assist the storm.

Gon. Nay, good, be patient.

Bo. When the sea is. Hence ! What cares these †
roarers for the name of king ?   To cabin ; silence ! trouble us not.

Gon. Good, yet remember whom thou hast aboard.

Bo. None that I more love than myself. You are a   **20**
counsellor, if you can command these elements to silence, and work the peace of the present, we will not hand a rope more, use your authority : if you cannot, give thanks you have liv'd so long, and make yourself ready in your cabin for the mischance of the hour, if it so hap.   Cheerly, good hearts ! Out of our way, I say.   *Exit*

Gon. I have great comfort from this fellow : methinks he hath no drowning mark upon him, his complexion is perfect gallows : stand fast, good Fate, to his   **30**
hanging, make the rope of his destiny our cable, for our own doth little advantage : if he be not born to be hang'd, our case is miserable.   *Exeunt*

Re-enter Boatswain

Bo. Down with the topmast ! yare, lower, lower, bring †
her to : try with main-course. (*A cry within.*) A

2

plague upon this howling! they are louder than
the weather, or our office.

Re-enter Sebastian, Antonio, and Gonzalo

Yet again? what do you here?   Shall we give o'er
and drown, have you a mind to sink?

Seb. A pox o' your throat, you bawling, blasphemous,   40
incharitable dog!

Bo. Work you then.

Ant. Hang, cur, hang, you whoreson insolent noise-
maker, we are less afraid to be drown'd than thou art.

Gon. I'll warrant him for drowning, though the ship were
no stronger than a nutshell, and as leaky as an
unstanched wench.

Bo. Lay her a-hold, a-hold set her two courses off to sea
again, lay her off.

Enter Mariners wet

Mar. All lost, to prayers, to prayers, all lost!   50

Bo. What, must our mouths be cold?

Gon. The king, and prince, at prayers! let's assist them, †
For our case is as theirs.

Seb.   I'm out of patience.

Ant. We are merely cheated of our lives by drunkards:
This wide-chopp'd rascal,—would thou might'st lie
    drowning
The washing of ten tides!

3

Gon.   He 'll be hang'd yet,
    Though every drop of water swear against it,
    And gape at wid'st to glut him.
    (*A confused noise within* : ' Mercy on us ! '—
    ' We split, we split ! '—' Farewell my wife and
        children ! '—   60
    ' Farewell, brother ! '—' We split, we split, we split ! ')

Ant. Let 's all sink with the king.

Seb. Let 's take leave of him.   *Exeunt Ant. and Seb.*

Gon. Now would I give a thousand furlongs of sea for
    an acre of barren ground ; long heath, brown firs, †
    any thing ; the wills above be done ; but I would
    fain die a dry death.   *Exeunt*

SCENE II

The island.   Before Prospero's cell

Enter Prospero and Miranda

Mir. If by your art, my dearest father, you 've
    Put the wild waters in this roar, allay them :
    The sky, it seems, would pour down stinking pitch,
    But that the sea, mounting to the welkin's cheek,
    Dashes the fire out.   O, I have suffer'd
    With those that I saw suffer ! a brave vessel,

(Who had no doubt some noble creature in her) †
Dash'd all to pieces !   O, the cry did knock
Against my very heart !   Poor souls, they perish'd.
Had I been any god of power, I would   10
Have sunk the sea within the earth, or ere
It should the good ship so have swallow'd, and
The fraughting souls within her.

Pro.   Be collected,
No more amazement : tell your piteous heart
There 's no harm done.

Mir.   O, woe the day !

Pro.   No harm.
I have done nothing but in care of thee,
(Of thee, my dear one, thee, my daughter) who
Art ignorant of what thou art, nought knowing
Of whence I am ; nor that I am more better
Than Prospero, master of a full poor cell,   20
And thy no greater father.

Mir.   More to know
Did never meddle with my thoughts.

Pro.   'Tis time
I should inform thee farther.   Lend thy hand,
And pluck my magic garment from me.—So,

                         Lays down his mantle

Lie there, my art : wipe thou thine eyes, have comfort,

5

The direful spectacle of the wreck, which touch'd
The very virtue of compassion in thee,
I have with such provision in mine art
So safely ordered, that there is no soïl,   †
No, not so much perdition as an hair,   30
Betid to any creature in the vessel
Which thou heard'st cry, which thou saw'st sink.
    Sit down,
For thou must now know farther.

Mir.   You have often
Begun to tell me what I am, but stopp'd
And left me to a bootless inquisition,
Concluding ' Stay : not yet.'

Pro.   The hour 's now come ;
The very minute bids thee ope thine ear,
Obey, and be attentive.   Canst thou remember
A time before we came unto this cell ?
I do not think thou canst, for then thou wast not   40
Out three years old.

Mir.   Certainly, sir, I can.

Pro. By what ? by any other house, or person ?
Of any thing the image tell me, that
Hath kept with thy remembrance.

Mir.   'Tis far off,
And rather like a dream, than an assurance

That my remembrance warrants.   Had I not
Four or five women once, that tended me ?

Pro. Thou hadst ; and more, Miranda.   But how is it
That this lives in thy mind ?   What seest thou else
In the dark backward and abysm of time ?   50
If thou remember'st aught ere thou cam'st here,
How thou cam'st here thou mayst.

Mir.   But that I do not.

Pro. Twelve year since, Miranda, twelve year since,
Thy father was the Duke of Milan and
A prince of power.

Mir.   Sir, are not you my father ?

Pro. Thy mother was a piece of virtue, and
She said thou wast my daughter ; and thy father
Was Duke of Milan, and his only heir
A princess, no worse issued.

Mir.   O the heavens,
What foul play had we, that we came from thence ?   60
Or blessed was 't we did ?

Pro.   Both, both, my girl.
By foul play (as thou say'st) were we heav'd thence,
But blessedly holp thither.

Mir.   O, my heart bleeds
To think o' the teen that I have turn'd you to,
Which is from my remembrance ! Please you, farther.

7

Pro. My brother and thy uncle, call'd Antonio,
 (I pray thee, mark me, that a brother should
 Be so perfidious!) he, whom next thyself
 Of all the world I lov'd, and to him put
 The manage of my state, as at that time   70
 Through all the signories it was the first,
 And Prospero the prime duke, being so reputed
 In dignity; and for the liberal arts
 Without a parallel; those being all my study,
 The government I cast upon my brother,
 And to my state grew stranger, being transported
 And rapt in secret studies, thy false uncle
 (Dost thou attend me?)

Mir.   Sir, most heedfully.

Pro. Being once perfected how to grant suits,
 How to deny them; who to advance, and who 80
 To trash for over-topping; new created
 The creatures that were mine, I say, or changed 'em,
 Or else new form'd 'em; having both the key,
 Of officer, and office, set all hearts i' the state
 To what tune pleas'd his ear, that now he was
 The ivy which had hid my princely trunk,
 And suck'd my verdure out on 't. Thou attend'st not.

Mir. O, good sir, I do.

Pro.   I pray thee, mark me.

I, thus neglecting worldly ends, all dedicated
To closeness, and the bettering of my mind   90
With that which, but by being so retir'd,   †
O'er-priz'd all popular rate, in my false brother
Awak'd an evil nature, and my trust,
Like a good parent, did beget of him
A falsehood in its contrary, as great
As my trust was, which had indeed no limit,
A confidence sans bound.   He being thus lorded,
Not only with what my revenue yielded,
But what my power might else exact, like one
Who having into truth, by telling of it,   †
Made such a sinner of his memory   101
To credit his own lie, he did believe
- He was indeed the duke, out o' the substitution
And executing the outward face of royalty
With all prerogative : hence his ambition growing,—
Dost thou hear ?

Mir.   Your tale, sir, would cure deafness.
Pro. To have no screen between this part he play'd
And him he play'd it for, he needs will be
Absolute Milan.   Me (poor man) my library
Was dukedom large enough : of temporal royalties   110
He thinks me now incapable ; confederates
(So dry he was for sway) wi' the King of Naples

To give him annual tribute, do him homage,
Subject his coronet to his crown, and bend
The dukedom yet unbow'd,—(alas, poor Milan !)
To most ignoble stooping.

Mir.   O the heavens !

Pro. Mark his condition, and the event, then tell me
If this might be a brother.

Mir.   I should sin
To think but nobly of my grandmother,
Good wombs have borne bad sons.

Pro.   Now the condition. 120
This King of Naples, being an enemy
To me inveterate, hearkens my brother's suit,
Which was, that he, in lieu o' the premises
Of homage, and I know not how much tribute,
Should presently extirpate me and mine
Out of the dukedom, and confer fair Milan,
With all the honours, on my brother : whereon,
A treacherous army levied, one midnight
Fated to the purpose, did Antonio open
The gates of Milan, and, i' the dead of darkness, 130
The ministers for the purpose hurried thence
Me, and thy crying self.

Mir.   Alack, for pity !
I, not remembering how I cried out then,

Will cry it o'er again : it is a hint
That wrings mine eyes to 't.

Pro.   Hear a little further.
And then I 'll bring thee to the present business
Which now 's upon 's ; without the which, this story
Were most impertinent.

Mir.   Wherefore did they not
That hour destroy us ?

Pro.   Well demanded, wench :
My tale provokes that question.   Dear, they durst not,
So dear the love my people bore me ; nor set   141
A mark so bloody on the business ; but
With colours fairer painted their foul ends.
In few, they hurried us aboard a bark,
Bore us some leagues to sea, where they prepar'd
A rotten carcass of a butt, not rigg'd,
Nor tackle, sail, nor mast, the very rats
Instinctively have quit it : there they hoist us,
To cry to the sea, that roar'd to us ; to sigh
To the winds, whose pity, sighing back again,   150
Did us but loving wrong.

Mir.   Alack, what trouble
Was I then to you !

Pro.   O, a cherubin
Thou wast that did preserve me ; thou didst smile,

Infused with a fortitude from heaven,
When I have deck'd the sea with drops full salt,   †
Under my burthen groan'd, which rais'd in me
An undergoing stomach, to bear up
Against what should ensue.

Mir.   How came we ashore ?

Pro. By Providence divine,
Some food we had, and some fresh water, that   **160**
A noble Neapolitan, Gonzalo,
Out of his charity, (who being then appointed
Master of this design) did give us, with
Rich garments, linens, stuffs, and necessaries,
Which since have steaded much ; so, of his gentleness,
Knowing I lov'd my books, he furnish'd me
From mine own library with volumes that
I prize above my dukedom.

Mir.   Would I might
But ever see that man !

Pro.   Now I arise,   *Resumes his mantle*
Sit still, and hear the last of our sea-sorrow :   **170**
Here in this island we arriv'd, and here
Have I, thy schoolmaster, made thee more profit
Than other princes can, that have more time
For vainer hours ; and tutors not so careful.

Mir. Heavens thank you for 't ! And now, I pray you, sir,

For still 'tis beating in my mind ; your reason
For raising this sea-storm ?

Pro.   Know thus far forth ;
By accident most strange, bountiful Fortune
(Now my dear lady) hath mine enemies
Brought to this shore ; and by my prescience   180
I find my zenith doth depend upon
A most auspicious star, whose influence
If now I court not, but omit, my fortunes
Will ever after droop.   Here cease more questions,
Thou art inclin'd to sleep ; 'tis a good dulness,
And give it way : I know thou canst not choose.

                                        Miranda sleeps

Come away, servant, come ; I am ready now,
Approach, my Ariel : come.

                        Enter Ariel

Ar. All hail, great master, grave sir, hail ! I come
To answer thy best pleasure ; be 't to fly,   190
To swim, to dive into the fire ; to ride
On the curl'd clouds ; to thy strong bidding, task
Ariel, and all his quality.

Pro.   Hast thou, spirit,
Perform'd to point the tempest that I bade thee ?

Ar. To every article.
    I boarded the king's ship ; now on the beak,

13

Now in the waist, the deck, in every cabin,
I flam'd amazement, sometime I 'ld divide
And burn in many places ; on the topmast,
The yards and bowsprit, would I flame distinctly,   200
Then meet, and join.   Jove's lightning, the precursors
O' the dreadful thunder-claps, more momentary
And sight-outrunning were not ; the fire, and cracks
Of sulphurous roaring, the most mighty Neptune
Seem'd to besiege, and make his bold waves tremble,
Yea, his dread trident shake.

Pro.   My brave spirit,
Who was so firm, so constant, that this coil
Would not infect his reason ?

Ar.   Not a soul
But felt a fever of the mad, and play'd   †
Some tricks of desperation ; all but mariners   210
Plung'd in the foaming brine, and quit the vessel, †
Then all afire with me : the king's son, Ferdinand,
With hair up-staring (then like reeds, not hair)
Was the first man that leap'd ; cried, ' Hell is empty,
And all the devils are here.'

Pro.   Why, that 's my spirit !
But was not this nigh shore ?

Ar.   Close by, my master.

Pro. But are they, Ariel, safe ?

Ar.   Not a hair perish'd ;
On their sustaining garments not a blemish,   †
But fresher than before : and as thou bad'st me
In troops I have dispers'd them 'bout the isle !   220
The king's son have I landed by himself,
Whom I left cooling of the air with sighs,
In an odd angle of the isle, and sitting   †
His arms in this sad knot.

Pro.   Of the king's ship,
The mariners, say how thou hast dispos'd,
And all the rest o' the fleet.

Ar.   Safely in harbour
Is the king's ship, in the deep nook, where once
Thou call'dst me up at midnight to fetch dew
From the still-vex'd Bermoothes, there she 's hid ; †
The mariners all under hatches stow'd,   230
Who, with a charm join'd to their suffer'd labour,
I have left asleep : and for the rest o' the fleet
(Which I dispers'd) they all have met again,
And are upon the Mediterranean flote
Bound sadly home for Naples,
Supposing that they saw the king's ship wreck'd,
And his great person perish.

Pro.   Ariel, thy charge
Exactly is perform'd ; but there 's more work :

What is the time o' the day?

Ar.   Past the mid season.

Pro. At least two glasses: the time 'twixt six and now   **240**
 Must by us both be spent most preciously.

Ar. Is there more toil? Since thou dost give me pains,
 Let me remember thee what thou hast promis'd,
 Which is not yet perform'd me.

Pro.   How now? moody?
 What is 't thou canst demand?

Ar.   My liberty.

Pro. Before the time be out? no more!

Ar.   I prithee,
 Remember I have done thee worthy service,
 Told thee no lies, made thee no mistakings, serv'd   †
 Without or grudge, or grumblings; thou didst promise
 To bate me a full year.

Pro.   Dost thou forget   **250**
 From what a torment I did free thee?

Ar.   No.

Pro. Thou dost: and think'st it much to tread the ooze
 Of the salt deep;
 To run upon the sharp wind of the north,
 To do me business in the veins o' the earth
 When it is bak'd with frost.

Ar.   I do not, sir.

16

Pro. Thou liest, malignant thing ! Hast thou forgot
    The foul witch Sycorax, who with age and envy
    Was grown into a hoop ? hast thou forgot her ?
Ar. No, sir.
Pro.   Thou hast : where was she born ? speak ; tell me. 260
Ar. Sir, in Argier.
Pro.   O, was she so ? I must   †
    Once in a month recount what thou hast been,
    Which thou forget'st. This damn'd witch Sycorax,
    For mischiefs manifold, and sorceries terrible
    To enter human hearing, from Argier
    Thou know'st was banish'd : for one thing she did
    They would not take her life : is not this true ?
Ar. Ay, sir.
Pro. This blue-eyed hag was hither brought with child,   †
    And here was left by the sailors ; thou my slave,   270
    As thou report'st thyself, was then her servant,
    And for thou wast a spirit too delicate
    To act her earthy and abhorr'd commands,
    Refusing her grand hests, she did confine thee,
    By help of her more potent ministers,
    And in her most unmitigable rage,
    Into a cloven pine, within which rift
    Imprison'd, thou didst painfully remain
    A dozen years : within which space she died,

   And left thee there : where thou didst vent thy groans
   As fast as mill-wheels strike : then was this island 281
   (Save for the son, that she did litter here,
   A freckled whelp, hag-born) not honour'd with
   A human shape.

Ar.   Yes ; Caliban her son.

Pro. Dull thing, I say so : he, that Caliban
   Whom now I keep in service ; thou best know'st
   What torment I did find thee in ; thy groans
   Did make wolves howl, and penetrate the breasts
   Of ever-angry bears ; it was a torment
   To lay upon the damn'd, which Sycorax   290
   Could not again undo : it was mine art,
   When I arriv'd, and heard thee, that made gape
   The pine, and let thee out.

Ar.   I thank thee, master.

Pro. If thou more murmur'st, I will rend an oak
   And peg thee in his knotty entrails, till
   Thou has howl'd away twelve winters.

Ar.   Pardon, master,
   I will be correspondent to command
   And do my spiriting gently.

Pro.   Do so : and after two days
   I will discharge thee.

Ar.   That 's my noble master !

What shall I do ? say what ; what shall I do ?   300

Pro. Go make thyself like a nymph o' the sea, be subject
To no sight but thine and mine ; invisible
To every eyeball else : go take this shape
And hither come in 't : go : hence with diligence !

                                        Exit Ariel

Awake, dear heart, awake, thou hast slept well ;
Awake !

Mir.   The strangeness of your story put
Heaviness in me.

Pro.   Shake it off : come on,
We 'll visit Caliban, my slave, who never
Yields us kind answer.

Mir.   'Tis a villain, sir,
I do not love to look on.

Pro.   But, as 'tis,   310
We cannot miss him : he does make our fire,
Fetch in our wood, and serves in offices
That profit us. What, ho ! slave ! Caliban !
Thou earth, thou ! speak.

Cal.   (*within*) There 's wood enough within.

Pro. Come forth, I say, there 's other business for thee :
Come, thou tortoise ! when ?

                Re-enter Ariel like a water-nymph

Fine apparition ! My quaint Ariel,

19

Hark in thine ear.

Ar. My lord, it shall be done. *Exit*

Pro. Thou poisonous slave, got by the devil himself
Upon thy wicked dam, come forth !   320

Enter Caliban

Cal. As wicked dew as e'er my mother brush'd
With raven's feather from unwholesome fen
Drop on you both ! a south-west blow on ye,
And blister you all o'er !

Pro. For this, be sure, to-night thou shalt have cramps,
Side-stitches, that shall pen thy breath up ; urchins
Shall, for that vast of night that they may work,
All exercise on thee ; thou shalt be pinch'd
As thick as honeycomb, each pinch more stinging
Than bees that made 'em.

Cal. I must eat my dinner :   330
This island's mine by Sycorax my mother,
Which thou tak'st from me.   When thou camest first,
Thou strok'st me, and made much of me ; wouldst
    give me
Water with berries in 't ; and teach me how
To name the bigger light, and how the less,
That burn by day, and night : and then I lov'd thee,
And show'd thee all the qualities o' th' isle,
The fresh springs, brine-pits, barren place and fertile :

Curs'd be I that I did so !   All the charms   †
Of Sycorax, toads, beetles, bats, light on you !   340
For I am all the subjects that you have,
Which first was mine own king: and here you sty me †
In this hard rock, whiles you do keep from me
The rest o' th' island.

Pro.   Thou most lying slave,
Whom stripes may move, not kindness ! I have us'd thee
(Filth as thou art) with human care, and lodg'd thee
In mine own cell, till thou didst seek to violate
The honour of my child.

Cal. O ho, O ho ! would 't had been done !
Thou didst prevent me ; I had peopled else   350
This isle with Calibans.

Pro.   Abhorred slave,   †
Which any print of goodness wilt not take,
Being capable of all ill ! I pitied thee,
Took pains to make thee speak, taught thee each hour
One thing or other : when thou didst not, savage,
Know thine own meaning, but wouldst gabble, like
A thing most brutish, I endow'd thy purposes
With words that make them known. But thy vile race
(Though thou didst learn) had that in 't which good
          natures
Could not abide to be with ; therefore wast thou   360

21

Deservedly confin'd into this rock, who hadst
Deserv'd more than a prison.

Cal. You taught me language, and my profit on 't
Is, I know how to curse. The red plague rid you
For learning me your language !

Pro.   Hag-seed, hence !
Fetch us in fuel and be quick thou 'rt best
To answer other business. Shrug'st thou, malice ?
If thou neglect'st, or dost unwillingly
What I command, I 'll rack thee with old cramps,
Fill all thy bones with aches, make thee roar,   370
That beasts shall tremble at thy din.

Cal.   No, pray thee.
(*aside*) I must obey, his art is of such power,
It would control my dam's god, Setebos,
And make a vassal of him.

Pro.   So, slave, hence ! *Exit Caliban*

*Re-enter Ariel, invisible, playing and singing ;
Ferdinand following*

ARIEL'S SONG

Come unto these yellow sands,
    And then take hands :
Courtsied when you have, and kiss'd   ✝
    The wild waves whist :

22

Foot it featly here and there;
And, sweet sprites, the burthen bear.   380
                    Hark, hark!
          Burthen (*dispersedly*). Bow-wow.
Ar. The watch dogs bark:
          Burthen (*dispersedly*). Bow-wow.
Ar. Hark, hark! I hear
          The strain of strutting chanticleer
          Cry, Cock-a-diddle-dow.

Fer. Where should this music be? i' th' air, or th' earth?
It sounds no more: and sure it waits upon
Some god o' th' island.   Sitting on a bank,
Weeping again the king my father's wreck,
This music crept by me upon the waters,   390
Allaying both their fury and my passion
With its sweet air: thence I have follow'd it,
(Or it hath drawn me rather) but 'tis gone.
No, it begins again.

                    Ariel sings

          Full fathom five thy father lies,
               Of his bones are coral made;
          Those are pearls that were his eyes,
               Nothing of him that doth fade,
          But doth suffer a sea-change

   Into something rich, and strange.   **400**
   Sea-nymphs hourly ring his knell :
      Burthen. Ding-dong

Ar. Hark ! now I hear them—Ding-dong, bell.

Fer. The ditty does remember my drown'd father ;
 This is no mortal business, nor no sound
 That the earth owes :—I hear it now above me.

Pro. The fringed curtains of thine eye advance,
 And say what thou seest yond.

Mir.   What is 't ? a spirit ?
 Lord, how it looks about ! Believe me, sir,
 It carries a brave form. But 'tis a spirit.   **410**

Pro. No, wench, it eats, and sleeps, and hath such senses
 As we have ; such. This gallant which thou seest
 Was in the wreck ; and, but he 's something stain'd
 With grief (that 's beauty's canker) thou mightest
  call him   †
 A goodly person : he hath lost his fellows,
 And strays about to find 'em.

Mir.   I might call him
 A thing divine, for nothing natural
 I ever saw so noble.

Pro.   (*aside*) It goes on, I see,
 As my soul prompts it : spirit, fine spirit, I 'll free thee

Within two days for this.

Fer.   Most sure the goddess   420
On whom these airs attend !   Vouchsafe my prayer
May know if you remain upon this island,
And that you will some good instruction give
How I may bear me here : my prime request
(Which I do last pronounce) is (O you wonder)
If you be maid, or no ?   †

Mir.   No wonder, sir,
But certainly a maid.

Fer.   My language ! heavens !
I am the best of them that speak this speech,
Were I but where 'tis spoken.

Pro.   How ? the best ?
What were thou, if the King of Naples heard thee ?   430

Fer. A single thing, as I am now, that wonders
To hear thee speak of Naples.   He does hear me ;
And that he does I weep : myself am Naples,
Who with mine eyes (never since at ebb) beheld
The king my father wreck'd.

Mir.   Alack, for mercy !

Fer. Yes, faith, and all his lords, the Duke of Milan
And his brave son being twain.   †

Pro.   (*aside*) The Duke of Milan,
And his more braver daughter, could control thee,

25

  If now 'twere fit to do 't. At the first sight
  They have chang'd eyes. Delicate Ariel,   440
  I 'll set thee free for this. (*to Fer.*) A word, good sir ; †
  I fear you have done yourself some wrong : a word.

Mir. Why speaks my father so ungently ? This
  Is the third man that e'er I saw ; the first
  That e'er I sigh'd for : pity move my father
  To be inclin'd my way !

Fer.   O, if a virgin,
  And your affection not gone forth, I 'll make you
  The queen of Naples.

Pro.   Soft, sir ! one word more.
  (*aside*) They are both in either's powers : but this
    swift business
  I must uneasy make, lest too light winning   450
  Make the prize light. (*to Fer.*) One word more ;
    I charge thee
  That thou attend me : thou dost here usurp
  The name thou ow'st not, and hast put thyself
  Upon this island as a spy, to win it
  From me, the lord on 't.

Fer.   No, as I am a man.

Mir. There 's nothing ill can dwell in such a temple :
  If the ill spirit have so fair a house,
  Good things will strive to dwell with 't.

Pro.   Follow me.
Speak not you for him ; he 's a traitor.   Come,
I 'll manacle thy neck and feet together :   460
Sea-water shalt thou drink ; thy food shall be
The fresh-brook mussels, wither'd roots, and husks
Wherein the acorn cradled.   Follow.

Fer.   No,
I will resist such entertainment, till
Mine enemy has more power.

                    He draws, and is charmed from moving
Mir.   O dear father,
Make not too rash a trial of him, for
He 's gentle, and not fearful.

Pro.   What ! I say,
My foot my tutor ?   Put thy sword up, traitor,
Who mak'st a show, but dar'st not strike ; thy
          conscience
Is so possess'd with guilt : come, from thy ward,   470
For I can here disarm thee with this stick,
And make thy weapon drop.

Mir.   Beseech you, father.

Pro. Hence ! hang not on my garments.

Mir.   Sir, have pity,
I 'll be his surety.

Pro.   Silence ! one word more

Shall make me chide thee, if not hate thee.   What ?
An advocate for an impostor ? hush !
Thou think'st there is no more such shapes as he,
(Having seen but him and Caliban :) foolish wench,
To the most of men this is a Caliban,
And they to him are angels.

Mir.   My affections   480
Are then most humble ; I have no ambition
To see a goodlier man.

Pro.   Come on, obey :
Thy nerves are in their infancy again,
And have no vigour in them.

Fer.   So they are :
My spirits, as in a dream, are all bound up :
My father's loss, the weakness which I feel,
The wreck of all my friends, nor this man's threats,
To whom I am subdued, are but light to me,
Might I but through my prison once a day
Behold this maid : all corners else o' th' earth   490
Let liberty make use of ; space enough
Have I in such a prison.

Pro.   (*aside*) It works.   (*to Fer.*) Come on.
Thou hast done well, fine Ariel !   (*to Fer.*) Follow me.
(*to Ar.*) Hark what thou else shalt do me.

Mir.   Be of comfort ;

My father's of a better nature, sir,
Than he appears by 'st† speech: this is unwonted
Which now came from him.
Pro.   Thou shalt be as free
As mountain winds; but then exactly do
All points of my command.
Ar.   To the syllable.
Pro. Come, follow: speak not for him.   *Exeunt* 500

Act Second

SCENE I

Another part of the island
Enter Alonso, Sebastian, Antonio, Gonzalo,
Adrian, Francisco, and others

Gon. Beseech you, sir, be merry; you have cause,
(So have we all) of joy; for our escape
Is much beyond our loss.   Our hint of woe
Is common, every day, some sailor's wife,
The masters of some merchant, and the merchant,
Have just our theme of woe; but for the miracle,
(I mean our preservation) few in millions

       Can speak like us : then wisely, good sir, weigh
       Our sorrow with our comfort.

Al.   Prithee, peace.

Seb. He receives comfort like cold porridge.   10

Ant. The visitor will not give him o'er so.

Seb. Look, he 's winding up the watch of his wit, by and
       by it will strike.

Gon. Sir,—

Seb. One : tell.

Gon. When every grief is entertain'd that 's offer'd,
       Comes to the entertainer—

Seb. A dollar.

Gon. Dolour comes to him, indeed, you have spoken truer
       than you purpos'd.   20

Seb. You have taken it wiselier than I meant you should.

Gon. Therefore, my lord,—

Ant. Fie, what a spendthrift is he of his tongue !

Al. I prithee spare.

Gon. Well, I have done : but yet,—

Seb. He will be talking.

Ant. Which, of he or Adrian, for a good wager, first begins
       to crow ?

Seb. The old cock.

Ant. The cockerel.   30

Seb. Done.   The wager ?

Ant. A laughter.

Seb. A match !

Adr. Though this island seem to be desert,—

Seb. Ha, ha, ha !—So ; you 're paid.

Adr. Uninhabitable, and almost inaccessible,—

Seb. Yet,—

Adr. Yet,—

Ant. He could not miss 't.

Adr. It must needs be of subtle, tender, and delicate   40
temperance.

Ant. Temperance was a delicate wench.

Seb. Ay, and a subtle, as he most learnedly deliver'd.

Adr. The air breathes upon us here most sweetly.

Seb. As if it had lungs, and rotten ones.

Ant. Or, as 'twere perfum'd by a fen.

Gon. Here is everything advantageous to life.

Ant. True, save means to live.

Seb. Of that there 's none, or little.

Gon. How lush and lusty the grass looks ! how green !   50

Ant. The ground, indeed, is tawny.

Seb. With an eye of green in 't.

Ant. He misses not much.

Seb. No ; he doth but mistake the truth totally.

Gon. But the rarity of it is, which is indeed almost beyond
credit,—

Seb. As many vouch'd rarities are.

Gon. That our garments, being, as they were, drench'd in the sea, hold notwithstanding their freshness and glosses, being rather new-dyed than stain'd with   60 salt water.

Ant. If but one of his pockets could speak, would it not say he lies ?

Seb. Ay, or very falsely pocket up his report.

Gon. Methinks our garments are now as fresh as when we put them on first in Afric, at the marriage of the king's fair daughter Claribel to the King of Tunis.

Seb. 'Twas a sweet marriage, and we prosper well in our return.

Adr. Tunis was never grac'd before with such a paragon   70 to their queen.

Gon. Not since widow Dido's time.   †

Ant. Widow ? a pox o' that ! How came that widow in ? widow Dido !

Seb. What if he had said ' widower Æneas ' too ? Good Lord, how you take it !

Adr. ' Widow Dido ' said you ? you make me study of that : she was of Carthage, not of Tunis.

Gon. This Tunis, sir, was Carthage.

Adr. Carthage ?   80

Gon. I assure you, Carthage.

Ant. His word is more than the miraculous harp.   †

Seb. He hath rais'd the wall. and houses too.

Ant. What impossible matter will he make easy next ?

Seb. I think he will carry this island home in his pocket,
    and give it his son for an apple.

Ant. And sowing the kernels of it in the sea, bring forth
    more islands.

Gon. Ay.   †

Ant. Why, in good time.   90

Gon. Sir, we were talking, that our garments seem now as
    fresh as when we were at Tunis at the marriage of
    your daughter, who is now queen.

Ant. And the rarest that e'er came there.

Seb. Bate, I beseech you, widow Dido.

Ant. O, widow Dido ? ay, widow Dido.

Gon. Is not, sir, my doublet as fresh as the first day I wore
    it ?   I mean, in a sort.

Ant. That sort was well fish'd for.

Gon. When I wore it at your daughter's marriage ?   100

Al. You cram these words into mine ears, against
    The stomach of my sense.   Would I had never
    Married my daughter there ! for, coming thence,
    My son is lost, and, in my rate, she too,
    Who is so far from Italy remov'd
    I ne'er again shall see her.   O thou mine heir

    Of Naples and of Milan, what strange fish
    Hath made his meal on thee ?

Fra.   Sir, he may live :   †
    I saw him beat the surges under him,
    And ride upon their backs ; he trod the water,   110
    Whose enmity he flung aside ; and breasted
    The surge most swoln that met him ; his bold head
    'Bove the contentious waves he kept, and oar'd
    Himself with his good arms in lusty stroke
    To the shore, that o'er his wave-worn basis bow'd,
    As stooping to relieve him : I not doubt
    He came alive to land :

Al.   No, no, he 's gone.

Seb. Sir, you may thank yourself for this great loss,
    That would not bless our Europe with your daughter,
    But rather loose her to an African ;   120
    Where she, at least, is banish'd from your eye,
    Who hath cause to wet the grief on 't.

Al.   Prithee peace.

Seb. You were kneel'd to, and importun'd otherwise,
    By all of us ; and the fair soul herself
    Weigh'd between loathness and obedience, at
    Which end o' the beam should bow.   We have lost
        your son,
    I fear for ever : Milan and Naples have

    Mo widows in them of this business' making
    Than we bring men to comfort them :
    The fault 's your own.

Al.   So is the dear'st o' the loss.   130

Gon. My lord Sebastian,
    The truth you speak doth lack some gentleness,
    And time to speak it in : you rub the sore,
    When you should bring the plaster.

Seb.   Very well.

Ant. And most chirurgeonly.

Gon. It is foul weather in us all, good sir.
    When you are cloudy.

Seb.   Foul weather ?

Ant.   Very foul.

Gon. Had I plantation of this isle, my lord,—

Ant. He 'ld sow 't with nettle-seed.

Seb.   Or docks, or mallows.

Gon. And were the king on 't, what would I do ?   140

Seb. 'Scape being drunk for want of wine.

Gon. I' the commonwealth I would by contraries
    Execute all things ; for no kind of traffic
    Would I admit ; no name of magistrate ;
    Letters should not be known ; riches, poverty,
    And use of service, none ; contract, succession,
    Bourn, bound of land, tilth, vineyard, none ;

  No use of metal, corn, or wine, or oil ;
  No occupation, all men idle, all ;
  And women too, but innocent and pure ;   150
  No sovereignty ;—

Seb.   Yet he would be king on 't.

Ant. The latter end of his commonwealth forgets the beginning.

Gon. All things in common nature should produce
  Without sweat or endeavour : treason, felony,
  Sword, pike, knife, gun, or need of any engine,
  Would I not have ; but nature should bring forth
  Of it own kind, all foison, all abundance,
  To feed my innocent people.

Seb. No marrying 'mong his subjects ?   160

Ant. None, man, all idle ; whores and knaves.

Gon. I would with such perfection govern, sir ;
  To excel the golden age.

Seb.   'Save his majesty !

Ant. Long live Gonzalo !

Gon.   And,—do you mark me, sir ?

Al. Prithee no more : thou dost talk nothing to me.

Gon. I do well believe your highness, and did it to minister occasion to these gentlemen, who are of such sensible and nimble lungs that they always use to laugh at nothing.

Ant. 'Twas you we laugh'd at.   170

Gon. Who in this kind of merry fooling am nothing to
you : so you may continue, and laugh at nothing
still.

Ant. What a blow was there given !

Seb. And it had not fallen flat-long.

Gon. You are gentlemen of brave mettle ; you would lift
the moon out of her sphere, if she would continue
in it five weeks without changing.

Enter Ariel (invisible) playing solemn music

Seb. We would so, and then go a bat-fowling.

Ant. Nay, good my lord, be not angry.   180

Gon. No.   I warrant you ; I will not adventure my dis-
cretion so weakly.   Will you laugh me asleep, for
I am very heavy ?

Ant. Go sleep, and hear us.

All sleep except Alonso, Sebastian, and Antonio

Al. What, all so soon asleep ?   I wish mine eyes
Would, with themselves, shut up my thoughts : I find
They are inclin'd to do so.

Seb.   Please you, sir,
Do not omit the heavy offer of it :
It seldom visits sorrow ; when it doth,
It is a comforter.

Ant.   We two, my lord,   190

37

    Will guard your person while you take your rest,
And watch your safety.

Al.   Thank you.—Wondrous heavy.

                      Alonso sleeps.   *Exit Ariel*

Seb. What a strange drowsiness possesses them !

Ant. It is the quality o' the climate.

Seb.   Why
Doth it not then our eyelids sink ?   I find not
Myself dispos'd to sleep.

Ant.   Nor I, my spirits are nimble.
They fell together all, as by consent
They dropp'd, as by a thunder-stroke.   What might,
Worthy Sebastian ?—O, what might ?—No more :—
And yet, methinks I see it in thy face,   200
What thou shouldst be : the occasion speaks thee, and
My strong imagination sees a crown
Dropping upon thy head.

Seb.   What ? art thou waking ?

Ant. Do you not hear me speak ?

Seb.   I do, and surely
It is a sleepy language ; and thou speak'st
Out of thy sleep.   What is it thou didst say ?
This is a strange repose, to be asleep
With eyes wide open ; standing, speaking, moving ;
And yet so fast asleep.

Ant.   Noble Sebastian,
      Thou let'st thy fortune sleep—die, rather ; wink'st   210
      Whiles thou art waking.
Seb.   Thou dost snore distinctly,
      There 's meaning in thy snores.
Ant. I am more serious than my custom : you
      Must be so too, if heed me ; which to do
      Trebles thee o'er.   †
Seb.   Well, I am standing water.
Ant. I 'll teach you how to flow.
Seb.   Do so : to ebb
      Hereditary sloth instructs me.
Ant.   O,
      If you but knew how you the purpose cherish
      Whiles thus you mock it ! how, in stripping it,
      You more invest it ! Ebbing men, indeed,   220
      (Most often) do so near the bottom run
      By their own fear, or sloth.
Seb.   Prithee say on :
      The setting of thine eye and cheek proclaim
      A matter from thee ; and a birth, indeed,
      Which throes thee much to yield.
Ant.   Thus, sir :
      Although this lord of weak remembrance, this,
      Who shall be of as little memory

    When he is earth'd, hath here almost persuaded
    (For he 's a spirit of persuasion, only
    Professes to persuade) the king his son 's alive,   230
    'Tis as impossible that he 's undrown'd,
    As he that sleeps here swims.

Seb.   I have no hope
    That he 's undrown'd.

Ant.   O, out of that ' no hope '
    What great hope have you ! no hope that way is
    Another way so high a hope that even
    Ambition cannot pierce a wink beyond,
    But doubt discovery there.   Will you grant with me †
    That Ferdinand is drown'd ?

Seb.   He 's gone.

Ant.   Then, tell me,
    Who 's the next heir of Naples ?

Seb.   Claribel.

Ant. She that is queen of Tunis ; she that dwells   240
    Ten leagues beyond man's life ; she that from Naples
    Can have no note, unless the sun were post,—
    The man i' the moon 's too slow,—till new-born chins
    Be rough and razorable ; she that from whom
    We all were sea-swallow'd, though some cast again,
    And (by that destiny) to perform an act
    Whereof what 's past is prologue ; what to come,

In yours and my discharge.

Seb.   What stuff is this ? how say you ?
'Tis true, my brother's daughter 's queen of Tunis ;
So is she heir of Naples, 'twixt which regions   250
There is some space.

Ant.   A space whose every cubit
Seems to cry out, ' How shall that Claribel
Measure us back to Naples ?   Keep in Tunis,
And let Sebastian wake.'   Say, this were death
That now hath seiz'd them, why, they were no worse
Than now they are.   There be that can rule Naples
As well as he that sleeps ; lords that can prate
As amply and unnecessarily
As this Gonzalo ; I myself could make
A chough of as deep chat.   O, that you bore   260
The mind that I do ! what a sleep were this
For your advancement !   Do you understand me ?

Seb. Methinks I do.

Ant.   And how does your content
Tender your own good fortune ?

Seb.   I remember
You did supplant your brother Prospero.

Ant.   True :
And look how well my garments sit upon me,
Much feater than before : my brother's servants

Were then my fellows, now they are my men.

Seb. But for your conscience?

Ant. Ay, sir; where lies that? if 'twere a kibe,   270
'Twould put me to my slipper: but I feel not
This deity in my bosom: twenty consciences,
That stand 'twixt me and Milan, candied be they,
And melt ere they molest! Here lies your brother,
No better than the earth he lies upon,
If he were that which now he 's like (that 's dead),
Whom I, with this obedient steel (three inches of it)
Can lay to bed for ever; whiles you, doing thus,
To the perpetual wink for aye might put
This ancient morsel, this Sir Prudence, who   280
Should not upbraid our course. For all the rest,
They 'll take suggestion, as a cat laps milk;
They 'll tell the clock to any business that
We say befits the hour.

Seb.   Thy case, dear friend,
Shall be my precedent; as thou got'st Milan,
I 'll come by Naples. Draw thy sword: one stroke
Shall free thee from the tribute which thou payest,
And I the king shall love thee.

Ant.   Draw together;
And when I rear my hand, do you the like,
To fall it on Gonzalo.

Seb.   O, but one word.   *They talk apart* 290
                    Re-enter Ariel, invisible

Ar. My master through his art foresees the danger
      That you, his friend, are in, and sends me forth
      (For else his project dies) to keep them living.
                              Sings in Gonzalo's ear

          While you here do snoring lie,
          Open-eyed conspiracy
                  His time doth take.
          If of life you keep a care,
          Shake off slumber and beware :
                  Awake, awake !

Ant. Then let us both be sudden.
Gon.   Now, good angels   300
      Preserve the king !   *They wake*
Al. Why, how now ? ho, awake ?—Why are you drawn ?
      Wherefore this ghastly looking ?
Gon.   What's the matter ?
Seb. Whiles we stood here securing your repose,
      Even now, we heard a hollow burst of bellowing
      Like bulls, or rather lions : did't not wake you ?
      It struck mine ear most terribly.
Al.   I heard nothing.
Ant. O, 'twas a din to fright a monster's ear ;

    To make an earthquake ! sure, it was the roar
    Of a whole herd of lions.

Al.   Heard you this, Gonzalo ? 310

Gon. Upon mine honour, sir, I heard a humming,
    And that a strange one too, which did awake me :
    I shak'd you, sir, and cried : as mine eyes open'd,
    I saw their weapons drawn :—there was a noise,
    That 's verily.   'Tis best we stand upon our guard ;
    Or that we quit this place : let 's draw our weapons.

Al. Lead off this ground and let 's make further search
    For my poor son.

Gon.   Heavens keep him from these beasts !
    For he is sure i' th' island.

Al.   Lead away.

Ar. Prospero my lord shall know what I have done ; 320
    So, king, go safely on to seek thy son.   *Exeunt*

SCENE II

Another part of the island

*Enter Caliban with a burden of wood. A noise
of thunder heard*

Cal. All the infections that the sun sucks up
    From bogs, fens, flats, on Prosper fall, and make him

By inch-meal a disease ! his spirits hear me,
And yet I needs must curse.   But they 'll nor pinch,
Fright me with urchin-shows, pitch me i' the mire,
Nor lead me, like a firebrand, in the dark
Out of my way, unless he bid 'em ; but
For every trifle are they set upon me,
Sometime like apes, that mow and chatter at me,
And after bite me ; then like hedgehogs, which   10
Lie tumbling in my barefoot way, and mount
Their pricks at my footfall ; sometime am I
All wound with adders, who with cloven tongues
Do hiss me into madness.

Enter Trinculo

　　　　Lo, now, lo !
Here comes a spirit of his, and to torment me
For bringing wood in slowly.   I 'll fall flat,
Perchance he will not mind me.

Tri. Here 's neither bush nor shrub, to bear off any
weather at all ; and another storm brewing, I hear
it sing i' the wind : yond same black cloud, yond   20
huge one, looks like a foul bombard that would shed
his liquor : if it should thunder as it did before,
I know not where to hide my head : yond same cloud
cannot choose but fall by pailfuls.   What have we
here, a man, or a fish ? dead or alive ?   A fish, he

smells like a fish ; a very ancient and fish-like smell ;
a kind of, not of the newest Poor-John.   A strange †
fish !   Were I in England now, as once I was, and
had but this fish painted, not a holiday fool there
but would give a piece of silver : there would this   30
monster make a man ; any strange beast there makes
a man : when they will not give a doit to relieve a
lame beggar, they will lay out ten to see a dead Indian.
Legg'd like a man ; and his fins like arms : warm o'
my troth : I do now let loose my opinion ; hold it
no longer : this is no fish, but an islander, that hath
lately suffered by a thunderbolt. (*Thunder*.) Alas, the
storm is come again ! my best way is to creep under
his gaberdine ; there is no other shelter hereabout :
misery acquaints a man with strange bed-fellows.   40
I will here shroud till the dregs of the storm be past.

Enter Stephano, singing : a bottle in his hand

Ste.   I shall no more to sea, to sea,
                           Here shall I die a-shore,—
This is a very scurvy tune to sing at a man's funeral :
well, here's my comfort.   *Drinks*
(*sings*)
        The master, the swabber, the boatswain, and I,
                The gunner, and his mate,

Lov'd Mall, Meg, and Marian, and Margery,
    But none of us car'd for Kate ;
    For she had a tongue with a tang,   50
    Would cry to a sailor, Go hang !
She lov'd not the savour of tar nor of pitch,
Yet a tailor might scratch her where'er she did itch.
    Then, to sea, boys, and let her go hang !
This is a scurvy tune too : but here's my comfort.

Drinks

Cal. Do not torment me :—O !

Ste. What's the matter ? Have we devils here ? Do
you put tricks upon 's with savages, and men of Ind,
ha ? I have not scap'd drowning, to be afeard now
of your four legs ; for it hath been said, As proper a   60
man as ever went on four legs cannot make him give
ground ; and it shall be said so again, while Stephano
breathes at nostrils.

Cal. The spirit torments me :—O !

Ste. This is some monster of the isle with four legs, who
hath got, as I take it, an ague. Where the devil
should he learn our language ? I will give him
some relief, if it be but for that : if I can recover
him, and keep him tame, and get to Naples with
him, he's a present for any emperor that ever trod   70
on neat's-leather.

Cal. Do not torment me, prithee ; I 'll bring my wood home faster.

Ste. He 's in his fit now ; and does not talk after the wisest ; he shall taste of my bottle : if he have never drunk wine afore, it will go near to remove his fit. If I can recover him, and keep him tame, I will not take too much for him ; he shall pay for him that hath him, and that soundly.

Cal. Thou dost me yet but little hurt ; thou wilt anon, I   80 know it by thy trembling : now Prosper works upon thee.

Ste. Come on your ways ; open your mouth ; here is that which will give language to you, cat : open †   your mouth ; this will shake your shaking, I can tell you, and that soundly : you cannot tell who 's your friend : open your chaps again.

Tri. I should know that voice : it should be—but he is drown'd ; and these are devils :—O defend me !

Ste. Four legs and two voices ; a most delicate monster !   90 His forward voice, now, is to speak well of his friend ; his backward voice is to utter foul speeches, and to detract. If all the wine in my bottle will recover him, I will help his ague. Come :—Amen ! I will pour some in thy other mouth.

Tri. Stephano !

Ste. Doth thy other mouth call me? Mercy, mercy! This is a devil, and no monster: I will leave him, I have no long spoon.

Tri. Stephano! If thou beest Stephano, touch me, and 100 speak to me; for I am Trinculo; be not afeard, thy good friend Trinculo.

Ste. If thou beest Trinculo, come forth: I'll pull thee by the lesser legs: if any be Trinculo's legs, these are they. Thou art very Trinculo indeed! How cam'st thou to be the siege of this moon-calf? can he vent Trinculos?

Tri. I took him to be killed with a thunder-stroke. But art thou not drown'd, Stephano? I hope, now, thou art not drown'd. Is the storm overblown? 110 I hid me under the dead moon-calf's gaberdine, for fear of the storm. And art thou living, Stephano? O Stephano, two Neapolitans scap'd!

Ste. Prithee, do not turn me about, my stomach is not constant.

Cal. (*aside*) These be fine things, an if they be not sprites. That's a brave god, and bears celestial liquor: I will kneel to him.

Ste. How didst thou scape? How cam'st thou hither? swear, by this bottle, how thou cam'st hither. I 120 escap'd upon a butt of sack, which the sailors

49

heaved o'erboard, by this bottle, which I made of the bark of a tree with mine own hands, since I was cast ashore.

Cal. I 'll swear upon that bottle, to be thy true subject, for the liquor is not earthly.

Ste. Here ; swear, then, how thou escapedst.

Tri. Swum ashore, man, like a duck : I can swim like a duck, I 'll be sworn.

Ste. Here, kiss the book.   Though thou canst swim like 130 a duck, thou art made like a goose.

Tri. O Stephano, hast any more of this ?

Ste. The whole butt, man : my cellar is in a rock by the sea-side, where my wine is hid.   How now, moon-calf, how does thine ague ?

Cal. Hast thou not dropp'd from heaven ?

Ste. Out o' the moon, I do assure thee : I was the man i' the moon, when time was.

Cal. I have seen thee in her ; and I do adore thee : my mistress show'd me thee, and thy dog, and thy bush. 140

Ste. Come, swear to that ; kiss the book : I will furnish it anon with new contents : swear.

Tri. By this good light, this is a very shallow monster ! I afeard of him ?   A very weak monster !   The man i' the moon ?   A most poor credulous monster ! Well drawn, monster, in good sooth !

Cal. I 'll show thee every fertile inch o' th' island ; and
    I will kiss thy foot : I prithee be my god.

Tri. By this light, a most perfidious and drunken monster !
    when 's god 's asleep, he 'll rob his bottle.   150

Cal. I 'll kiss thy foot ; I 'll swear myself thy subject.

Ste. Come on, then ; down, and swear.

Tri. I shall laugh myself to death at this puppy-headed
    monster. A most scurvy monster ! I could find
    in my heart to beat him,—

Ste. Come, kiss.

Tri. But that the poor monster 's in drink. An abomin-
    able monster !

Cal. I 'll show thee the best springs ; I 'll pluck thee
      berries ;
    I 'll fish for thee ; and get thee wood enough.   160
    A plague upon the tyrant that I serve !
    I 'll bear him no more sticks, but follow thee,
    Thou wondrous man.

Tri. A most ridiculous monster, to make a wonder of a
    poor drunkard !

Cal. I prithee let me bring thee where crabs grow ;
    And I with my long nails will dig thee pig-nuts ;
    Show thee a jay's nest, and instruct thee how
    To snare the nimble marmoset ; I 'll bring thee
    To clustering filberts, and sometimes I 'll get thee   170

Young scamels from the rock. Wilt thou go with †
   me ?

Ste. I prithee now lead the way without any more talking.
Trinculo, the king and all our company else being
drown'd, we will inherit here : here ; bear my
bottle : fellow Trinculo, we 'll fill him by and by †
again.

Cal. (*sings drunkenly*)

      Farewell, master ; farewell, farewell !

Tri. A howling monster ; a drunken monster !

Cal.

      No more dams I 'll make for fish,

      Nor fetch in firing   180

         At requiring ;

      Nor scrape trencher, nor wash dish :   †

      'Ban, 'Ban, Ca-caliban

      Has a new master :—get a new man.

Freedom, hey-day ! hey-day, freedom ! freedom,
hey-day, freedom !

Ste. O brave monster ! Lead the way.   *Exeunt*

Act Third

SCENE I

Before Prospero's cell

Enter Ferdinand, bearing a log

Fer. There be some sports are painful, and their labour
  Delight in them sets off : some kinds of baseness
  Are nobly undergone ; and most poor matters
  Point to rich ends.   This my mean task
  Would be as heavy to me as odious, but
  The mistress which I serve quickens what 's dead,
  And makes my labours pleasures : O, she is
  Ten times more gentle than her father 's crabbed ;
  And he 's compos'd of harshness.   I must remove
  Some thousands of these logs, and pile them up,   10
  Upon a sore injunction : my sweet mistress
  Weeps when she sees me work, and says, such baseness
  Had never like executor.   I forget :
  But these sweet thoughts do even refresh my labours,
  Most busy lest, when I do it.   †

  Enter Miranda ; and Prospero at a distance, unseen

Mir.   Alas, now, pray you,

53

Work not so hard : I would the lightning had
Burnt up those logs that you are enjoin'd to pile !
Pray set it down, and rest you : when this burns,
'Twill weep for having wearied you : my father
Is hard at study ; pray now rest yourself,   20
He 's safe for these three hours.

Fer.   O most dear mistress,
The sun will set before I shall discharge
What I must strive to do.

Mir.   If you 'll sit down,
I 'll bear your logs the while : pray give me that,
I 'll carry it to the pile.

Fer.   No, precious creature,
I had rather crack my sinews, break my back,
Than you should such dishonour undergo,
While I sit lazy by.

Mir.   It would become me
As well as it does you ; and I should do it
With much more ease ; for my good will is to it,   30
And yours it is against.

Pro.   Poor worm, thou art infected !
This visitation shows it.

Mir.   You look wearily.

Fer. No, noble mistress, 'tis fresh morning with me   †
When you are by at night.   I do beseech you,—

54

Chiefly that I might set it in my prayers,—
What is your name ?

Mir.   Miranda.—O my father,
I have broke your hest to say so !

Fer.   Admir'd Miranda,
Indeed the top of admiration, worth
What 's dearest to the world !   Full many a lady
I have ey'd with best regard, and many a time   40
The harmony of their tongues hath into bondage
Brought my too diligent ear : for several virtues
Have I lik'd several women, never any
With so full soul, but some defect in her
Did quarrel with the noblest grace she ow'd,
And put it to the foil : but you, O you,
So perfect, and so peerless, are created
Of every creature's best !

Mir.   I do not know
One of my sex ; no woman's face remember,
Save, from my glass, mine own ; nor have I seen   50
More that I may call men than you, good friend,
And my dear father : how features are abroad
I am skilless of ; but, by my modesty
(The jewel in my dower) I would not wish
Any companion in the world but you ;
Nor can imagination form a shape,

      Besides yourself, to like of.   But I prattle
      Something too wildly, and my father's precepts
      I therein do forget.

Fer.   I am, in my condition,
      A prince, Miranda, I do think, a king,   60
      (I would not so) and would no more endure
      This wooden slavery than to suffer
      The flesh-fly blow my mouth.   Hear my soul speak :
      The very instant that I saw you, did
      My heart fly to your service, there resides
      To make me slave to it, and for your sake
      Am I this patient log-man.

Mir.   Do you love me ?

Fer. O heaven, O earth, bear witness to this sound,
      And crown what I profess with kind event
      If I speak true ! if hollowly, invert   70
      What best is boded me to mischief !   I,
      Beyond all limit of what else i' the world,
      Do love, prize, honour you.

Mir.   I am a fool
      To weep at what I am glad of.

Pro.   Fair encounter
      Of two most rare affections !   Heavens rain grace
      On that which breeds between 'em !

Fer.   Wherefore weep you ?

Mir. At mine unworthiness, that dare not offer
    What I desire to give ; and much less take
    What I shall die to want.   But this is trifling,
    And all the more it seeks to hide itself,   80
    The bigger bulk it shows.   Hence, bashful cunning,
    And prompt me, plain and holy innocence !
    I am your wife, if you will marry me ;
    If not, I'll die your maid : to be your fellow
    You may deny me, but I'll be your servant
    Whether you will or no.

Fer.   My mistress, dearest,
    And I thus humble ever.

Mir.   My husband, then ?

Fer. Ay, with a heart as willing
    As bondage e'er of freedom : here's my hand.

Mir. And mine, with my heart in't : and now farewell   90
    Till half an hour hence.

Fer.   A thousand thousand !
         Exeunt Ferdinand and Miranda severally

Pro. So glad of this as they I cannot be,
    Who are surpris'd withal ; but my rejoicing
    At nothing can be more.   I'll to my book,
    For yet ere supper-time must I perform
    Much business appertaining.   *Exit*

SCENE II

Another part of the Island

Enter Caliban, Stephano, and Trinculo

Ste. Tell not me ;—when the butt is out, we will drink
water, not a drop before : therefore bear up, and
board 'em. Servant-monster, drink to me.

Tri. Servant-monster ? the folly of this island ! They †
say there 's but five upon this isle ; we are three of
them, if th' other two be brain'd like us, the state
totters.

Ste. Drink, servant-monster, when I bid thee, thy eyes are
almost set in thy head.

Tri. Where should they be set else ? he were a brave   10
monster indeed, if they were set in his tail.

Ste. My man-monster hath drown'd his tongue in sack :
for my part, the sea cannot drown me, I swam, ere I
could recover the shore, five-and-thirty leagues off
and on, by this light, thou shalt be my lieutenant
monster, or my standard.

Tri. Your lieutenant, if you list, he 's no standard.

Ste. We 'll not run, Monsieur Monster.

Tri. Nor go neither ; but you 'll lie like dogs, and yet
say nothing neither.   20

58

Ste. Moon-calf, speak once in thy life, if thou beest a
good moon-calf.

Cal. How does thy honour ?   Let me lick thy shoe.   I 'll
not serve him, he is not valiant.

Tri. Thou liest, most ignorant monster, I am in case to
justle a constable.   Why, thou debosh'd fish thou,
was there ever man a coward, that hath drunk so
much sack as I to-day ?   Wilt thou tell a monstrous
lie, being but half a fish, and half a monster ?

Cal. Lo, how he mocks me !   wilt thou let him, my lord ?   30

Tri. ' Lord,' quoth he ?   That a monster should be such
a natural !

Cal. Lo, lo, again !   bite him to death, I prithee.

Ste. Trinculo, keep a good tongue in your head :   if you
prove a mutineer, the next tree !   The poor monster 's my subject, and he shall not suffer indignity.

Cal. I thank my noble lord.   Wilt thou be pleas'd to
hearken once again to the suit I made to thee ?

Ste. Marry, will I :   kneel, and repeat it ;   I will stand, and
so shall Trinculo.   40

Enter Ariel, invisible

Cal. As I told thee before, I am subject to a tyrant, a
sorcerer, that by his cunning hath cheated me of
the island.

Ar. Thou liest.

Cal. Thou liest, thou jesting monkey, thou :
    I would my valiant master would destroy thee !
    I do not lie.

Ste. Trinculo, if you trouble him any more in 's tale, by
    this hand, I will supplant some of your teeth.

Tri. Why, I said nothing.   50

Ste. Mum then, and no more.   Proceed.

Cal. I say, by sorcery he got this isle ;
    From me he got it.   If thy greatness will
    Revenge it on him, (for I know thou darest
    But this thing dare not,)

Ste. That 's most certain.

Cal. Thou shalt be lord of it, and I 'll serve thee.

Ste. How now shall this be compass'd ?   Canst thou
    bring me to the party ?

Cal. Yea, yea, my lord, I 'll yield him thee asleep,   60
    Where thou mayst knock a nail into his head.

Ar. Thou liest, thou canst not.

Cal. What a pied ninny 's this !   Thou scurvy patch !
    I do beseech thy greatness give him blows,
    And take his bottle from him : when that 's gone,
    He shall drink nought but brine, for I 'll not show him
    Where the quick freshes are.

Ste. Trinculo, run into no further danger : interrupt the
    monster one word further, and, by this hand, I 'll

turn my mercy out o' doors, and make a stock-fish   70
of thee.

Tri. Why, what did I ? I did nothing. I 'll go farther
off.

Ste. Didst thou not say he lied ?

Ar. Thou liest.

Ste. Do I so ? take thou that. (*Beats him.*) As you like
this, give me the lie another time.

Tri. I did not give the lie. Out o' your wits, and hear-
ing too ? A pox o' your bottle ! this can sack and
drinking do. A murrain on your monster, and the   80
devil take your fingers !

Cal. Ha, ha, ha !

Ste. Now, forward with your tale.—Prithee, stand farther
off.

Cal. Beat him enough : after a little time,
I 'll beat him too.

Ste.   Stand farther : come, proceed.

Cal. Why, as I told thee, 'tis a custom with him
I' th' afternoon to sleep : there thou mayst brain him,
Having first seiz'd his books ; or with a log
Batter his skull, or paunch him with a stake,   90
Or cut his wezand with thy knife. Remember
First to possess his books ; for without them
He 's but a sot, as I am, nor hath not

One spirit to command : they all do hate him
As rootedly as I.   Burn but his books.
He has brave utensils (for so he calls them)
Which, when he has a house, he 'll deck withal.
And that most deeply to consider is
The beauty of his daughter ; he himself
Calls her a nonpareil : I never saw a woman,   100
But only Sycorax my dam, and she ;
But she as far surpasseth Sycorax
As great'st does least.

Ste.   Is it so brave a lass ?

Cal. Ay, lord, she will become thy bed, I warrant,
And bring thee forth brave brood.

Ste. Monster, I will kill this man : his daughter and I
will be king and queen,—save our graces !—and
Trinculo and thyself shall be viceroys.   Dost thou
like the plot, Trinculo ?

Tri. Excellent.   110

Ste. Give me thy hand, I am sorry I beat thee ; but, while
thou liv'st, keep a good tongue in thy head.

Cal. Within this half hour will he be asleep,
Wilt thou destroy him then ?

Ste.   Ay, on mine honour

Ar. This will I tell my master.

Cal. Thou mak'st me merry ; I am full of pleasure,

Let us be jocund : will you troll the catch
You taught me but while-ere ?

Ste. At thy request, monster, I will do reason, any reason,
—Come on, Trinculo, let us sing.   *Sings* 120

   Flout 'em and scout 'em,   †
   And scout 'em and flout 'em ;
    Thought is free.

Cal. That 's not the tune.

    Ariel plays the tune on a tabor and pipe

Ste. What is this same ?

Tri. This is the tune of our catch, play'd by the picture
of Nobody.

Ste. If thou beest a man, show thyself in thy likeness :
if thou beest a devil, tak 't as thou list.

Tri. O, forgive me my sins !   130

Ste. He that dies pays all debts : I defy thee.   Mercy
upon us !

Cal. Art thou afeard ?

Ste. No, monster, not I.

Cal. Be not afeard, the isle is full of noises,
Sounds, and sweet airs, that give delight, and hurt not :
Sometimes a thousand twangling instruments
Will hum about mine ears ; and sometime voices,
That, if I then had wak'd after long sleep,
Will make me sleep again, and then, in dreaming,   140

     The clouds methought would open, and show riches
     Ready to drop upon me, that, when I wak'd,
     I cried to dream again.

Ste. This will prove a brave kingdom to me, where
     I shall have my music for nothing.

Cal. When Prospero is destroy'd.

Ste. That shall be by and by : I remember the story.

Tri. The sound is going away, let 's follow it, and after
     do our work.

Ste. Lead, monster, we 'll follow. I would I could see   150
     this taborer, he lays it on.

Tri. Wilt come ? I 'll follow, Stephano.   *Exeunt*

SCENE III

Another part of the island

*Enter Alonso, Sebastian, Antonio, Gonzalo, Adrian,
Francisco, and others*

Gon. By 'r lakin, I can go no further, sir,
     My old bones ache : here 's a maze trod, indeed,
     Through forth-rights, and meanders ! By your patience,
     I needs must rest me.

Al.   Old lord, I cannot blame thee,
     Who am myself attach'd with weariness,

To the dulling of my spirits : sit down, and rest :
Even here I will put off my hope, and keep it
No longer for my flatterer : he is drown'd
Whom thus we stray to find, and the sea mocks
Our frustrate search on land. Well, let him go.   10

Ant. (*aside to Seb.*) I am right glad that he 's so out of hope :
Do not, for one repulse, forego the purpose
That you resolv'd to effect.

Seb.   (*aside to Ant.*) The next advantage
Will we take thoroughly.

Ant.   (*aside to Seb.*) Let it be to-night,
For, now they are oppress'd with travel, they
Will not, nor cannot use such vigilance
As when they are fresh.

Seb.   (*aside to Ant.*) I say to-night : no more.

                    Solemn and strange music

Al. What harmony is this ?—My good friends, hark !
Gon. Marvellous sweet music !

*Enter Prospero above, invisible. Enter several strange Shapes,
    bringing in a banquet : they dance about it with gentle
    actions of salutations ; and, inviting the King, &c. to
    eat, they depart*

Al. Give us kind keepers, heavens !—What were these ?   20
Seb. A living drollery. Now I will believe
That there are unicorns ; that in Arabia

65

  There is one tree, the phœnix' throne, one phœnix
  At this hour reigning there.
Ant.   I 'll believe both ;
  And what does else want credit, come to me,
  And I 'll be sworn 'tis true : travellers ne'er did lie,
  Though fools at home condemn 'em.
Gon.   If in Naples
  I should report this now, would they believe me ?
  If I should say, I saw such islanders,
  (For, certes, these are people of the island,)   **30**
  Who, though they are of monstrous shape, yet,
    note,
  Their manners are more gentle-kind than of
  Our human generation you shall find
  Many, nay, almost any.
Pro.   (*aside*) Honest lord,
  Thou hast said well ; for some of you there present
  Are worse than devils.
Al.   I cannot too much muse
  Such shapes, such gesture, and such sound, expressing
  (Although they want the use of tongue) a kind
  Of excellent dumb discourse.
Pro.   (*aside*) Praise in departing.
Fra. They vanish'd strangely.
Seb.   No matter, since   **40**

They have left their viands behind ; for we have
    stomachs.

Will 't please you taste of what is here ?

Al.   Not I.

Gon. Faith, sir, you need not fear. When we were boys,
    Who would believe that there were mountaineers
    Dew-lapp'd like bulls, whose throats had hanging †
      at 'em
    Wallets of flesh ? or that there were such men
    Whose heads stood in their breasts ? which now
      we find.
    Each putter-out of five for one will bring us
    Good warrant of.

Al.   I will stand to, and feed,
    Although my last, no matter, since I feel   50
    The best is past. Brother, my lord the duke,
    Stand to, and do as we.

*Thunder and lightning. Enter Ariel, like a harpy ; claps his
    wings upon the table ; and, with a quaint device, the
    banquet vanishes*

Ar. You are three men of sin, whom Destiny,
    That hath to instrument this lower world,
    And what is in 't, the never-surfeited sea
    Hath caus'd to belch up you ; and on this island,
    Where man doth not inhabit, you 'mongst men

Being most unfit to live. I have made you mad ;
And even with such-like valour men hang and drown
Their proper selves.

Alonso, Sebastian, &c. draw their swords

You fools, I and my fellows   60
Are ministers of Fate, the elements,
Of whom your swords are temper'd, may as well
Wound the loud winds, or with bemock'd-at stabs
Kill the still-closing waters, as diminish
One dowle that's in my plume : my fellow-ministers
Are like invulnerable. If you could hurt,
Your swords are now too massy for your strengths,
And will not be uplifted. But remember
(For that's my business to you) that you three
From Milan did supplant good Prospero,   70
Expos'd unto the sea (which hath requit it)
Him and his innocent child : for which foul deed,
The powers, delaying (not forgetting) have
Incens'd the seas and shores ; yea, all the creatures,
Against your peace. Thee of thy son, Alonso,
They have bereft ; and do pronounce by me
Lingering perdition (worse than any death
Can be at once) shall step by step attend
You and your ways, whose wraths to guard you from,
Which here, in this most desolate isle, else falls   80

Upon your heads, is nothing but heart's-sorrow,
And a clear life ensuing.

*He vanishes in thunder ; then, to soft music, enter the Shapes
again, and dance, with mocks and mows, and carrying out
the table*

Pro. Bravely the figure of this harpy hast thou
 Perform'd, my Ariel ; a grace it had, devouring :   †
 Of my instruction hast thou nothing bated
 In what thou hadst to say : so, with good life
 And observation strange, my meaner ministers
 Their several kinds have done : my high charms work,
 And these mine enemies are all knit up
 In their distractions : they now are in my power ;   90
 And in these fits I leave them, while I visit
 Young Ferdinand (whom they suppose is drown'd)
 And his and mine lov'd darling.   *Exit above*

Gon. I' the name of something holy, sir, why stand you
 In this strange stare ?

Al.   O, it is monstrous ! monstrous !
 Methought the billows spoke, and told me of it,
 The winds did sing it to me ; and the thunder
 (That deep and dreadful organ-pipe) pronounc'd
 The name of Prosper : it did bass my trespass,
 Therefore my son i' th' ooze is bedded ; and   100
 I 'll seek him deeper than e'er plummet sounded,

69

And with him there lie mudded.   *Exit*

Seb.   But one fiend at a time,
I 'll fight their legions o'er.

Ant.   I 'll be thy second.

                Exeunt Sebastian and Antonio

Gon. All three of them are desperate : their great guilt
    (Like poison given to work a great time after)
    Now 'gins to bite the spirits.   I do beseech you   †
    (That are of suppler joints) follow them swiftly,
    And hinder them from what this ecstasy
    May now provoke them to.

Adr.   Follow, I pray you.   *Exeunt*

Act Fourth

SCENE I

Before Prospero's cell

Enter Prospero, Ferdinand, and Miranda

Pro. If I have too austerely punish'd you,
    Your compensation makes amends, for I
    Have given you here a third of mine own life,   †
    Or that for which I live ; who once again

I tender to thy hand : all thy vexations
Were but my trials of thy love, and thou
Hast strangely stood the test : here, afore Heaven,
I ratify this my rich gift.   O Ferdinand,
Do not smile at me, that I boast her off,   †
For thou shalt find she will outstrip all praise,   10
And make it halt behind her.

Fer.   I do believe it
Against an oracle.

Pro. Then, as my gift, and thine own acquisition
Worthily purchas'd, take my daughter : but
If thou dost break her virgin-knot, before
All sanctimonious ceremonies may
With full and holy rite be minister'd,
No sweet aspersion shall the heavens let fall
To make this contract grow ; but barren hate,
Sour-eyed disdain, and discord shall bestrew   20
The union of your bed, with weeds so loathly
That you shall hate it both : therefore take heed,
As Hymen's lamps shall light you.

Fer.   As I hope
For quiet days, fair issue and long life,
With such love as 'tis now, the murkiest den,
The most opportune place, the strong'st suggestion
Our worser genius can, shall never melt

71

Mine honour into lust, to take away
The edge of that day's celebration,
When I shall think, or Phœbus' steeds are founder'd,   30
Or Night kept chain'd below.

Pro.   Fairly spoke ;
Sit, then, and talk with her, she is thine own.
What, Ariel ! my industrious servant, Ariel !

Enter Ariel

Ar. What would my potent master ? here I am.

Pro. Thou, and thy meaner fellows, your last service
Did worthily perform ; and I must use you
In such another trick.   Go bring the rabble
(O'er whom I give thee power) here to this place :
Incite them to quick motion, for I must
Bestow upon the eyes of this young couple   40
Some vanity of mine art : it is my promise,
And they expect it from me.

Ar.   Presently ?

Pro. Ay, with a twink.

Ar.   Before you can say, ' come,' and ' go,'
And breathe twice, and cry, ' so, so,'
Each one, tripping on his toe,
Will be here with mop and mow.
Do you love me, master ? no ?

Pro. Dearly, my delicate Ariel.   Do not approach

72

Till thou dost hear me call.

Ar.   Well ; I conceive. *Exit* 50

Pro. Look thou be true ; do not give dalliance
Too much the rein : the strongest oaths are straw
To the fire i' the blood : be more abstemious,
Or else, good night your vow !

Fer.   I warrant you, sir,
The white cold virgin snow upon my heart
Abates the ardour of my liver.

Pro.   Well.
Now come, my Ariel ! bring a corollary,
Rather than want a spirit : appear, and pertly !
No tongue ! all eyes ! be silent.   *Soft music*

Enter Iris

Iris. Ceres, most bounteous lady, thy rich leas   60
Of wheat, rye, barley, vetches, oats, and pease ;
Thy turfy mountains, where live nibbling sheep,
And flat meads thatch'd with stover, them to keep ;
Thy banks with pioned and twilled brims,   †
Which spongy April at thy hest betrims,
To make cold nymphs chaste crowns ; and thy
          broom-groves,
Whose shadow the dismissed bachelor loves,
Being lass-lorn ; thy pole-clipt vineyard ;
And thy sea-marge, sterile and rocky-hard,

73

Where thou thyself dost air ;—the queen o' the sky, 70
Whose watery arch and messenger am I,
Bids thee leave these, and with her sovereign grace,
Here, on this grass-plot, in this very place,
To come and sport :—her peacocks fly amain :

Juno appears in her car above

Approach, rich Ceres, her to entertain.

Enter Ceres

Cer. Hail, many-colour'd messenger, that ne'er
Dost disobey the wife of Jupiter ;
Who, with thy saffron wings, upon my flowers
Diffusest honey-drops, refreshing showers,
And with each end of thy blue bow dost crown 80
My bosky acres and my unshrubb'd down,
Rich scarf to my proud earth ;—why hath thy queen
Summon'd me hither, to this short-grass'd green ?

Iris. A contract of true love to celebrate,
And some donation freely to estate
On the bless'd lovers.

Cer.   Tell me, heavenly bow,
If Venus or her son, as thou dost know,
Do now attend the queen ?   Since they did plot
The means that dusky Dis my daughter got,   †
Her, and her blind boy's scandal'd company,   90
I have forsworn.

74

Iris.   Of her society
        Be not afraid : I met her deity
        Cutting the clouds towards Paphos ; and her son
        Dove-drawn with her : here thought they to have done
        Some wanton charm upon this man and maid,
        Whose vows are, that no bed-right shall be paid
        Till Hymen's torch be lighted : but in vain ;
        Mars's hot minion is return'd again,
        Her waspish-headed son has broke his arrows,
        Swears he will shoot no more, but play with sparrows,
        And be a boy right out.

Cer.   High'st queen of state,   101
        Great Juno, comes ; I know her by her gait.

                    Enter Juno

Juno. How does my bounteous sister ?   Go with me
        To bless this twain, that they may prosperous be,
        And honour'd in their issue.   *They sing :*

Juno.   Honour, riches, marriage-blessing,
              Long continuance, and increasing,
              Hourly joys be still upon you !
              Juno sings her blessings on you.

Cer.   Earth's increase, foison plenty,   †
              Barns and garners never empty ;   111
              Vines with clustering bunches growing ;

> Plants with goodly burthen bowing ;
> Spring come to you at the farthest
> In the very end of harvest !
> Scarcity and want shall shun you ;
> Ceres' blessing so is on you.

Fer. This is a most majestic vision, and
Harmonious charmingly.   May I be bold
To think these spirits ?

Pro.   Spirits, which by mine art   120
I have from their confines call'd to enact
My present fancies.

Fer.   Let me live here ever ;
So rare a wonder'd father and a wise   †
Makes this place Paradise.

> *Juno and Ceres whisper, and send*
> *Iris on employment*

Pro.   Sweet, now, silence !
Juno and Ceres whisper seriously ;
There 's something else to do : hush, and be mute,
Or else our spell is marr'd.

Iris. You nymphs call'd Naiads of the windring brooks,
With your sedg'd crowns, and ever-harmless looks,
Leave your crisp channels, and on this green land   130
Answer your summons ; Juno does command :

Come, temperate nymphs, and help to celebrate
A contract of true love ; be not too late.

Enter certain Nymphs

You sunburn'd sicklemen, of August weary,
Come hither from the furrow, and be merry,
Make holiday ; your rye-straw hats put on,
And these fresh nymphs encounter every one
In country footing.

Enter certain Reapers, properly habited : they join with the
Nymphs in a graceful dance ; towards the end whereof
Prospero starts suddenly, and speaks ; after which, to a
strange, hollow, and confused noise, they heavily vanish.

Pro. (*aside*) I had forgot that foul conspiracy
Of the beast Caliban and his confederates   140
Against my life : the minute of their plot
Is almost come.   (*to the Spirits*) Well done ! avoid ;
    no more !

Fer. This is strange : your father's in some passion
That works him strongly.

Mir.   Never till this day
Saw I him touch'd with anger, so distemper'd.

Pro. You do look, my son, in a moved sort,   †
As if you were dismay'd : be cheerful, sir.
Our revels now are ended.   These our actors,
(As I foretold you) were all spirits, and

77

    Are melted into air, into thin air,   150
    And like the baseless fabric of this vision,
    The cloud-capp'd towers, the gorgeous palaces,
    The solemn temples, the great globe itself,
    Yea, all which it inherit, shall dissolve,   †
    And like this insubstantial pageant faded,
    Leave not a rack behind : we are such stuff
    As dreams are made on ; and our little life
    Is rounded with a sleep.   Sir, I am vex'd,
    Bear with my weakness, my old brain is troubled :
    Be not disturb'd with my infirmity ;   160
    If you be pleas'd, retire into my cell,
    And there repose, a turn or two I 'll walk,
    To still my beating mind.

Fer. Mir.   We wish your peace. *Exeunt*
Pro. Come with a thought.   I thank thee, Ariel : come. †

Enter Ariel

Ar. Thy thoughts I cleave to, what 's thy pleasure ?
Pro.   Spirit,
    We must prepare to meet with Caliban.
Ar. Ay, my commander, when I presented Ceres,
    I thought to have told thee of it, but I fear'd
    Lest I might anger thee.
Pro. Say again, where didst thou leave these varlets ?   170
Ar. I told you, sir, they were red-hot with drinking,

So full of valour, that they smote the air
For breathing in their faces ; beat the ground
For kissing of their feet ; yet always bending
Towards their project.   Then I beat my tabor,
At which like unback'd colts they prick'd their ears,
Advanc'd their eyelids, lifted up their noses
As they smelt music, so I charm'd their ears,
That, calf-like, they my lowing follow'd, through
Tooth'd briers, sharp furzes, pricking goss, and
    thorns,   180
Which enter'd their frail shins ; at last I left them
I' the filthy-mantled pool beyond your cell,
There dancing up to the chins, that the foul lake
O'erstunk their feet.   †

Pro.   This was well done, my bird.
Thy shape invisible retain thou still :
The trumpery in my house, go bring it hither,
For stale to catch these thieves.

Ar.   I go, I go.   *Exit*

Pro. A devil, a born devil, on whose nature
Nurture can never stick ; on whom my pains,
Humanely taken, all, all lost, quite lost ;   190
And as with age his body uglier grows,
So his mind cankers.   I will plague them all,
Even to roaring.

Re-enter Ariel, loaden with glistering apparel, &c.
Come, hang them on this line.
Prospero and Ariel remain, invisible
Enter Caliban, Stephano, and Trinculo, all wet

Cal. Pray you, tread softly, that the blind mole may not
Hear a foot fall : we now are near his cell.

Ste. Monster, your fairy, which you say is a harmless fairy,
has done little better than play'd the Jack with us.

Tri. Monster, I do smell all horse-piss, at which my nose
is in great indignation. 200

Ste. So is mine. Do you hear, monster ? If I should
take a displeasure against you, look you,—

Tri. Thou wert but a lost monster.

Cal. Good my lord, give me thy favour still,
Be patient, for the prize I 'll bring thee to
Shall hoodwink this mischance : therefore speak softly,
All 's hush'd as midnight yet.

Tri. Ay, but to lose our bottles in the pool,—

Ste. There is not only disgrace and dishonour in that,
monster, but an infinite loss. 210

Tri. That 's more to me than my wetting : yet this is
your harmless fairy, monster.

Ste. I will fetch off my bottle, though I be o'er ears for
my labour.

Cal. Prithee, my king, be quiet. See'st thou here,

This is the mouth o' the cell : no noise, and enter :
Do that good mischief, which may make this island
Thine own for ever, and I, thy Caliban,
For aye thy foot-licker.

Ste. Give me thy hand. I do begin to have bloody 220
thoughts.

Tri. O King Stephano !   O peer !   O worthy Stephano !
look what a wardrobe here is for thee !

Cal. Let it alone, thou fool, it is but trash.

Tri. O, ho, monster ! we know what belongs to a frippery.
O King Stephano !

Ste. Put off that gown, Trinculo, by this hand, I 'll have
that gown.

Tri. Thy grace shall have it.

Cal. The dropsy drown this fool ! what do you mean   230
To dote thus on such luggage ?   Let 's alone,   †
And do the murder first : if he awake,
From toe to crown he 'll fill our skins with pinches,
Make us strange stuff.

Ste. Be you quiet, monster.   Mistress line, is not this †
my jerkin ?   Now is the jerkin under the line : now,
jerkin, you are like to lose your hair, and prove a bald
jerkin.

Tri. Do, do ; we steal by line and level, an 't like your †
grace.   240

81

Ste. I thank thee for that jest; here's a garment for 't :
wit shall not go unrewarded while I am king of this
country. 'Steal by line and level' is an excellent
pass of pate; there's another garment for 't.

Tri. Monster, come, put some lime upon your fingers,
and away with the rest.

Cal. I will have none on 't : we shall lose our time,
And all be turn'd to barnacles, or to apes
With foreheads villanous low.

Ste. Monster, lay-to your fingers : help to bear this away 250
where my hogshead of wine is, or I 'll turn you out
of my kingdom : go to, carry this.

Tri. And this.

Ste. Ay, and this.

*A noise of hunters heard. Enter divers Spirits, in shape of
dogs and hounds, hunting them about ; Prospero and
Ariel setting them on*

Pro. Hey, Mountain, hey !

Ar. Silver ! there it goes, Silver !

Pro. Fury, Fury ! there, Tyrant, there ! hark, hark !
     Caliban, Stephano, and Trinculo are driven out
Go, charge my goblins that they grind their joints
With dry convulsions, shorten up their sinews
With aged cramps, and more pinch-spotted make them
Than pard or cat o' mountain.

Ar.   Hark, they roar !

Pro. Let them be hunted soundly.   At this hour
        Lies at my mercy all mine enemies :
        Shortly shall all my labours end, and thou
        Shalt have the air at freedom : for a little
        Follow, and do me service.   *Exeunt*

Act Fifth

SCENE I

Before the cell of Prospero

Enter Prospero, in his magic robes, and Ariel

Pro. Now does my project gather to a head :
        My charms crack not ; my spirits obey, and time
        Goes upright with his carriage.   How 's the day ?

Ar. On the sixth hour, at which time, my lord,
        You said our work should cease.

Pro.   I did say so,
        When first I rais'd the tempest : say, my spirit,
        How fares the king, and 's followers ?

Ar.   Confin'd together
        In the same fashion as you gave in charge,

Just as you left them ; all prisoners, sir,
In the line-grove which weather-fends your cell ;   10
They cannot budge till your release.   The king,
His brother, and yours, abide all three distracted,
And the remainder mourning over them,
Brimful of sorrow and dismay ; but chiefly
Him that you term'd, sir, ' The good old lord,
    Gonzalo ' ;
His tears runs down his beard, like winter's drops
From eaves of reeds.   Your charm so strongly
    works 'em,
That if you now beheld them, your affections
Would become tender.

Pro.   Dost thou think so, spirit ?
Ar. Mine would, sir, were I human.
Pro.   And mine shall.   20
Hast thou (which art but air) a touch, a feeling
Of their afflictions, and shall not myself,
One of their kind, that relish all as sharply,
Passion as they, be kindlier mov'd than thou art ?
Though with their high wrongs I am struck to the
    quick,
Yet with my nobler reason 'gainst my fury
Do I take part : the rarer action is
In virtue than in vengeance : they being penitent,

The sole drift of my purpose doth extend
Not a frown further.   Go, release them, Ariel,   30
My charms I 'll break, their senses I 'll restore,
And they shall be themselves.

Ar.   I 'll fetch them, sir. *Exit*

Pro. Ye elves of hills, brooks, standing lakes, and groves,
And ye, that on the sands with printless foot
Do chase the ebbing Neptune, and do fly him
When he comes back ; you demi-puppets, that
By moonshine do the green sour ringlets make,
Whereof the ewe not bites ; and you, whose pastime
Is to make midnight mushrooms, that rejoice
To hear the solemn curfew, by whose aid   40
(Weak masters though ye be) I have bedimm'd
The noontide sun, call'd forth the mutinous winds,
And 'twixt the green sea, and the azur'd vault
Set roaring war : to the dread rattling thunder
Have I given fire, and rifted Jove's stout oak
With his own bolt ; the strong-bas'd promontory
Have I made shake, and by the spurs pluck'd up
The pine and cedar : graves at my command
Have wak'd their sleepers, op'd, and let 'em forth
By my so potent art.   But this rough magic   50
I here abjure ; and, when I have requir'd
Some heavenly music (which even now I do)

To work mine end upon their senses, that
This airy charm is for, I 'll break my staff,
Bury it certain fathoms in the earth,
And deeper than did ever plummet sound
I 'll drown my book.   *Solemn music*

*Re-enter Ariel before: then Alonso, with a frantic
gesture, attended by Gonzalo; Sebastian and Antonio
in like manner attended by Adrian and Francisco: they
all enter the circle which Prospero had made, and there
stand charmed; which Prospero observing, speaks:*

A solemn air, and the best comforter
To an unsettled fancy, cure thy brains   59
(Now useless) boil within thy skull! There stand,   †
For you are spell-stopp'd.   †
Holy Gonzalo, honourable man,
Mine eyes, even sociable to the show of thine,
Fall fellowly drops.   The charm dissolves apace;
And as the morning steals upon the night,
Melting the darkness, so their rising senses
Begin to chase the ignorant fumes that mantle
Their clearer reason.   O good Gonzalo,
My true preserver, and a loyal sir
To him thou follow'st! I will pay thy graces   70
Home both in word and deed.   Most cruelly
Didst thou, Alonso, use me and my daughter:

Thy brother was a furtherer in the act.
Thou art pinch'd for 't now, Sebastian.   Flesh and
  blood,
You, brother mine, that entertain'd ambition,
Expell'd remorse and nature, who, with Sebastian
(Whose inward pinches therefore are most strong)
Would here have kill'd your king ; I do forgive thee,
Unnatural though thou art.   Their understanding
Begins to swell, and the approaching tide   80
Will shortly fill the reasonable shore,
That now lies foul and muddy.   Not one of them
That yet looks on me, or would know me : Ariel,
Fetch me the hat and rapier in my cell,
I will discase me, and myself present
As I was sometime Milan : quickly, spirit,
Thou shalt ere long be free.

Ariel sings and helps to attire him
  Where the bee sucks, there suck I,
  In a cowslip's bell I lie,
  There I couch when owls do cry.   90
  On the bat's back I do fly
  After summer merrily.
  Merrily, merrily shall I live now
  Under the blossom that hangs on the bough.

Pro. Why, that 's my dainty Ariel ! I shall miss thee ;
But yet thou shalt have freedom : so, so, so.
To the king's ship, invisible as thou art,
There shalt thou find the mariners asleep
Under the hatches ; the master and the boatswain
Being awake, enforce them to this place,   100
And presently, I prithee.

Ar. I drink the air before me, and return
Or ere your pulse twice beat.   *Exit*

Gon. All torment, trouble, wonder and amazement
Inhabits here : some heavenly power guide us
Out of this fearful country !

Pro.   Behold, sir king,
The wronged Duke of Milan, Prospero :
For more assurance that a living prince
Does now speak to thee, I embrace thy body ;
And to thee and thy company I bid   110
A hearty welcome.

Al.   Whe'er thou be'st he or no,
Or some enchanted trifle to abuse me,
(As late I have been) I not know : thy pulse
Beats, as of flesh and blood ; and, since I saw thee,
The affliction of my mind amends, with which,
I fear'd, a madness held me : this must crave—
An if this be at all—a most strange story.

Thy dukedom I resign, and do entreat
Thou pardon me my wrongs.—But how should Prospero
Be living, and be here ?

Pro.   First, noble friend,   120
Let me embrace thine age, whose honour cannot
Be measur'd or confin'd.

Gon.   Whether this be
Or be not, I 'll not swear.

Pro.   You do yet taste
Some subtilties o' the isle, that will not let you
Believe things certain.   Welcome, my friends all !
(*aside to Seb. and Ant.*) But you, my brace of lords,
          were I so minded,
I here could pluck his highness' frown upon you,
And justify you traitors : at this time
I will tell no tales.

Seb.   (*aside*) The devil speaks in him.

Pro.   No.
For you, most wicked sir, whom to call brother   130
Would even infect my mouth, I do forgive
Thy rankest fault,—all of them ; and require
My dukedom of thee, which perforce, I know,
Thou must restore.

Al.   If thou be 'st Prospero,

89

  Give us particulars of thy preservation,
  How thou hast met us here, who three hours since
  Were wreck'd upon this shore ; where I have lost—
  How sharp the point of this remembrance is !—
  My dear son Ferdinand.

Pro.   I am woe for 't, sir.

Al. Irreparable is the loss, and patience   140
  Says it is past her cure.

Pro.   I rather think
  You have not sought her help, of whose soft grace
  For the like loss I have her sovereign aid,
  And rest myself content.

Al.   You the like loss ?

Pro. As great to me, as late ; and, supportable   †
  To make the dear loss, have I means much weaker
  Than you may call to comfort you ; for I
  Have lost my daughter.

Al.   A daughter ?
  O heavens, that they were living both in Naples,
  The king and queen there ! that they were, I wish 150
  Myself were mudded in that oozy bed
  Where my son lies. When did you lose your
    daughter ?

Pro. In this last tempest. I perceive these lords
  At this encounter do so much admire,

That they devour their reason, and scarce think
Their eyes do offices of truth, their words
Are natural breath : but, howsoe'er you have
Been justled from your senses, know for certain
That I am Prospero, and that very duke
Which was thrust forth of Milan, who most strangely 160
Upon this shore, where you were wreck'd, was landed,
To be the lord on 't.   No more yet of this,
For 'tis a chronicle of day by day,
Not a relation for a breakfast, nor
Befitting this first meeting.   Welcome, sir ;
This cell 's my court : here have I few attendants,
And subjects none abroad : pray you look in.
My dukedom since you have given me again,
I will requite you with as good a thing,
At least bring forth a wonder, to content ye   170
As much as me my dukedom.

   Here Prospero discovers Ferdinand and Miranda,
       playing at chess

Mir. Sweet lord, you play me false.

Fer.   No, my dear'st love,
I would not for the world.

Mir. Yes, for a score of kingdoms you should wrangle, †
And I would call it fair play.

Al.   If this prove

  A vision of the island, one dear son
  Shall I twice lose.

Seb.   A most high miracle !
Fer. Though the seas threaten, they are merciful.
  I have curs'd them without cause.   *Kneels*
Al.   Now all the blessings
  Of a glad father compass thee about !   180
  Arise, and say how thou cam'st here.
Mir.   O, wonder !
  How many goodly creatures are there here !
  How beauteous mankind is ! O brave new world,
  That has such people in 't !
Pro.   'Tis new to thee.
Al. What is this maid, with whom thou wast at play ?
  Your eld'st acquaintance cannot be three hours :
  Is she the goddess that hath sever'd us,
  And brought us thus together ?
Fer.   Sir, she is mortal ;
  But, by immortal Providence, she 's mine ;
  I chose her when I could not ask my father 190
  For his advice ; nor thought I had one. She
  Is daughter to this famous Duke of Milan,
  Of whom so often I have heard renown,
  But never saw before ; of whom I have
  Receiv'd a second life ; and second father

This lady makes him to me.

Al.   I am hers :
But, O, how oddly will it sound, that I
Must ask my child forgiveness !

Pro.   There, sir, stop,
Let us not burthen our remembrance with
A heaviness that 's gone.

Gon.   I have inly wept,   200
Or should have spoke ere this. Look down, you gods,
And on this couple drop a blessed crown !
For it is you that have chalk'd forth the way
Which brought us hither.

Al.   I say, Amen, Gonzalo !

Gon. Was Milan thrust from Milan, that his issue
Should become kings of Naples ?   O, rejoice
Beyond a common joy, and set it down
With gold on lasting pillars : In one voyage
Did Claribel her husband find at Tunis,
And Ferdinand, her brother, found a wife   210
Where he himself was lost ; Prospero his dukedom
In a poor isle ; and all of us ourselves,
When no man was his own.

Al.   (*to Fer. and Mir.*) Give me your hands :
Let grief and sorrow still embrace his heart
That doth not wish you joy !

Gon.   Be it so ! Amen !

Re-enter Ariel, with the Master and Boatswain
amazedly following

O, look, sir, look, sir ! here is more of us :
I prophesied, if a gallows were on land,
This fellow could not drown.   Now, blasphemy,
That swear'st grace o'erboard, not an oath on shore ?
Hast thou no mouth by land ?   What is the news ?   **220**

Bo.   The best news is, that we have safely found
Our king and company ; the next, our ship—
Which, but three glasses since, we gave out split—
Is tight, and yare, and bravely rigg'd, as when
We first put out to sea.

Ar.   (*aside to Pro.*) Sir, all this service
Have I done since I went.

Pro.   (*aside to Ar.*) My tricksy spirit !

Al.   These are not natural events, they strengthen
From strange to stranger : say, how came you hither ?

Bo.   If I did think, sir, I were well awake,
I 'ld strive to tell you.   We were dead of sleep,   **230**
And (how we know not) all clapp'd under hatches,
Where, but even now, with strange and several noises
Of roaring, shrieking, howling, jingling chains,
And mo diversity of sounds, all horrible,
We were awak'd ; straightway, at liberty ;

Where we, in all her trim, freshly beheld
Our royal, good, and gallant ship ; our master
Capering to eye her :—on a trice, so please you,
Even in a dream, were we divided from them,
And were brought moping hither.

Ar.   (*aside to Pro.*) Was 't well done ? 240

Pro. (*aside to Ar.*) Bravely, my diligence ; thou shalt be
   free.

Al. This is as strange a maze as e'er men trod,
   And there is in this business more than nature
   Was ever conduct of : some oracle
   Must rectify our knowledge.

Pro.   Sir, my liege,
   Do not infest your mind with beating on
   The strangeness of this business ; at pick'd leisure
   (Which shall be shortly single) I 'll resolve you,
   Which to you shall seem probable, of every   250
   These happen'd accidents ; till when, be cheerful,
   And think of each thing well.   (*aside to Ariel*) Come
       hither, spirit,
   Set Caliban, and his companions free ;
   Untie the spell. (*exit Ariel.*) How fares my gracious
       sir ?
   There are yet missing of your company
   Some few odd lads that you remember not.

Re-enter Ariel, driving in Caliban, Stephano, and
Trinculo, in their stolen apparel

Ste. Every man shift for all the rest, and let no man take
care of himself ; for all is but fortune.—Coragio,
bully-monster, coragio !

Tri. If these be true spies which I wear in my head, here 's 260
a goodly sight.

Cal. O Setebos, these be brave spirits indeed !
How fine my master is !   I am afraid
He will chastise me.

Seb.   Ha, ha !
What things are these, my lord Antonio ?
Will money buy 'em ?

Ant.   Very like ; one of them
Is a plain fish, and, no doubt, marketable.

Pro. Mark but the badges of these men, my lords,
Then say if they be true.   This mis-shapen knave,
His mother was a witch, and one so strong   270
That could control the moon ; make flows, and ebbs,
And deal in her command, without her power.
These three have robb'd me, and this demi-devil
(For he 's a bastard one) had plotted with them
To take my life.   Two of these fellows you
Must know and own, this thing of darkness I
Acknowledge mine.

Cal.   I shall be pinch'd to death.

Al. Is not this Stephano, my drunken butler ?

Seb. He is drunk now ; where had he wine ?

Al. And Trinculo is reeling ripe : where should they   280
    Find this grand liquor that hath gilded 'em ?
    How cam'st thou in this pickle ?

Tri. I have been in such a pickle since I saw you last, that
    I fear me will never out of my bones : I shall not fear
    fly-blowing.

Seb. Why, how now, Stephano ?

Ste. O, touch me not ;—I am not Stephano, but a cramp.

Pro. You 'ld be king o' the isle, sirrah ?

Ste. I should have been a sore one, then.

Al. This is a strange thing as e'er I look'd on.   290

                      Pointing to Caliban

Pro. He is as disproportion'd in his manners
    As in his shape.   Go, sirrah, to my cell,
    Take with you your companions ; as you look
    To have my pardon, trim it handsomely.

Cal. Ay, that I will ; and I 'll be wise hereafter,
    And seek for grace.   What a thrice-double ass
    Was I to take this drunkard for a god,
    And worship this dull fool !

Pro.   Go to, away !

Al. Hence, and bestow your luggage where you found it.

Seb. Or stole it, rather.   300

                         Exeunt Caliban, Stephano, and Trinculo

Pro. Sir, I invite your Highness, and your train
   To my poor cell ; where you shall take your rest
   For this one night, which, part of it, I 'll waste
   With such discourse as, I not doubt, shall make it
   Go quick away : the story of my life,
   And the particular accidents gone by
   Since I came to this isle : and in the morn
   I 'll bring you to your ship, and so to Naples,
   Where I have hope to see the nuptial
   Of these our dear-belov'd solemnized,   310
   And thence retire me to my Milan, where
   Every third thought shall be my grave.

Al.   I long
   To hear the story of your life ; which must
   Take the ear strangely.

Pro.   I 'll deliver all,
   And promise you calm seas, auspicious gales,
   And sail so expeditious, that shall catch
   Your royal fleet far off. (*aside to Ariel*) My Ariel,
       chick,
   That is thy charge : then to the elements
   Be free, and fare thou well ! Please you, draw near.

                                              Exeunt

EPILOGUE

Spoken by Prospero

Now my charms are all o'erthrown,
And what strength I have 's mine own,
Which is most faint : now, 'tis true,
I must be here confin'd by you,
Or sent to Naples.   Let me not,
Since I have my dukedom got,
And pardon'd the deceiver, dwell
In this bare island by your spell,
But release me from my bands
With the help of your good hands :   10
Gentle breath of yours my sails
Must fill, or else my project fails,
Which was to please.   Now I want
Spirits to enforce, art to enchant ;
And my ending is despair,
Unless I be reliev'd by prayer,
Which pierces so, that it assaults
Mercy itself, and frees all faults.
As you from crimes would pardon'd be,
Let your indulgence set me free.   20

Notes

I. i. 1. *Boatswain*; F gives this spelling every time but one, in l. 12, where it reads *Boson*. The New Cambridge editors assume the latter to be Shakespeare's own spelling, regularised all but once by the compositor. It is to be hoped that everyone will pronounce the word *Bos'n* however spelt, and the matter is therefore of small importance; but to read *Bos'n* everywhere except in l. 10, there retaining *Boatswain* ' as befitting the speech of a king ' (thus New Cambridge) seems to me one of the oddities of editing, as though one should insist on one's king saying Chol-mon-de-ley, but allow the rest of one's characters the accepted Chumley.

I. i. 7. *Blow till thou burst thy wind*; addressing the storm (and nothing to do with the whistle!); see note on l. 34.

I. i. 16. *cares*; 'compositor's grammar,' say the New Cambridge editors, regularising to *care* with Rowe; but why not boatswain's, or rather bos'n's, grammar? Or even Shakespeare's?

I. i. 34. *bring her to: try with main course*; F reads *bring her to Try with . . .* (It is worth observing in passing that the New Cambridge editors, who so strongly hold the F punctuation and capitalisations of this play up for our admiration and study, take no notice of the capital T, and readily omit a full-stop later. It is of course quite arguable that the compositor was no seaman, and was mystified, but the whole argument for attention to F's punctuation depends on a belief in the compositor's fidelity to his copy, and his fidelity ought to be more rather than less exact when he is puzzled.) There is an excellent discussion of the seamanship of this scene in *Shakespeare's England*, I. 161-62, though one point in it seems to me difficult to square with the text. And the whole

business is worth studying, since it is not merely a vague stage
hurly-burly of a storm, but a perfectly coherent account of an
attempt to save a ship. The general situation is clear; there is a
violent storm, and the ship is on a lee-shore. The storm in itself
is nothing to bother about (*Blow till thou burst thy wind, if room
enough*); that is merely a question of easing the ship, first by
lowering the topsail (there being in those days no reefs) and then
lowering the top-mast. The next thing is to bring her to, *i.e.* to
bring her head to sea and wind and only just so much off the wind
as will keep her diminished sail filling and herself under control.
This position was known as 'trying' or 'lying a-try,' and I think
that the F punctuation may be justified, as two separate orders,
'bring her to' and then 'let her lie "a-try"' under mainsail only.
In this position a ship would ride out any storm easily in the open
sea. But she would also drift to leeward, which in the open would
not matter, but on a lee-shore is perilous, since she is not carrying
enough sail to claw off the shore, and the point will come where
whatever the risk more sail must be set, to give her not merely
steerage-way, but a positive forward movement into the wind
and off the shore. And hence the order in l. 48. No one has
explained what, if anything, *lay her a-hold* means. The term seems
to be unknown, and *Shakespeare's England* is perhaps right in
assuming that this should be 'lay her a-hull,' *i.e.* head to wind,
with no sail set. But I think that *Shakespeare's England* is clearly
wrong in assuming this order to be an independent one, followed
by an interval ('It soon appears that if she continues to hull the
ship will go ashore'). The three directions are all orders for one
consecutive operation; to facilitate the setting of the two courses
(the equivalent of reefed foresail and mainsail) the ship must
momentarily be brought head to wind: the courses are then set:

the ship's head is then thrown 'off' the wind, so that the sails will draw. In ll. 48, 49 I have retained F's punctuation. The ordinary reading is *set her two courses. Off to sea again*, the second part of which sounds to me an oddly 'landsmanly' phrase, and if we are to tinker I would rather read *set her two courses; off* (*i.e.* a shorter order for 'lay her off'); *to sea again; lay her off*. I have gone into this scene at some length, because it is so easy to miss the tense (and, if one may put it so, film-like) effectiveness of the technical sequence of events.

I. i. 52. *The king, and prince, at prayers;* the F stage-directions for this scene are muddled. After the general entry of Alonso, Ferdinand, and the rest, the only exit (apart from the boatswain's) is for Gonzalo, though the entry of Sebastian and Antonio with him at l. 38 implies that they also had gone off. I imagine that at l. 33 they all go off, and that Alonso and Ferdinand are supposed to be still in their cabins at their prayers.

I. i. 65. *brown firs;* F *firrs,* for which most editors read *furze,* even if they do not follow the more drastic Hanmer to *ling, heath, broom, furse.*

I. ii. 7. 'The bracket (F) is a revelation here. Miranda is fey, and the spell of the "noble creature" (Ferdinand) is already upon her' (New Cambridge). I see no reason to suppose that Miranda is fey, and the F bracket is a perfectly normal typographical device for indicating an amplifying, but to the sense unnecessary, comment.

I. ii. 29. *soil;* so Johnson, for F's *soule.* I think that the New Cambridge editors are almost certainly right in accepting this emendation. They have been criticised for reluctance to accept the anacoluthon otherwise produced; there are of course plenty of anacolutha in Shakespeare; but Prospero is in no sort of excitement or disorder of mind; on the contrary he is explaining with calm satisfaction how well his schemes have worked; and a violent anacoluthon would be undramatic.

I. ii. 91. *With that which, but by being so retir'd . . .*; there seems to be here a compression of thought amounting almost to confusion. As the sentence stands it means 'that which (*i.e.* study) was of more value than popular estimation except that it was so retired,' with some doubt whether *popular rate* means 'popularity' or 'the people's judgment of values.'

I. ii. 100. *into truth*; to justify their emendation *minted* for *into* the New Cambridge editors have a long note, which seems to me more ingenious than convincing. The general sense is clear; 'by repeatedly telling it he has made his lie seem to himself a truth, so that even his memory is false to the facts.' I do not think it is impossible to extract that sense even from the text as we have it; but if we are to suspect corruption I should be more inclined to suppose that the compositor got muddled with two versions in which the deletions were imperfectly indicated: *e.g.* two such versions as

> *Who having into truth, by telling of it,*
> *Converted his own lie,*

and

> *Who having, by the often telling of it*
> *Made such a sinner of his memory*
> *To credit his own lie,*

(I do not of course suggest that this is what *did* happen, but only that it is the sort of thing that in such cases *may* happen).

I. ii. 155. *deck'd*; an odd word; the New Cambridge editors would read *eked*, saying that *deck'd* is usually explained as 'sprinkled,' but that O.E.D. gives no support for that. True; but no one, I imagine, supposes that one can write an equation ' deck = sprinkle ': if Shakespeare wrote *deck'd* it is no more than one of his frequent rather forced metaphors. But *eked* is not much less forced, and the parallel adduced from *The Merchant of Venice* does not help matters at all, since the sense there is natural, of time, *to eke it, and to draw it out in length* (III. ii. 23) ; time can be eked out as the sea cannot be.

I. ii. 209. *fever of the mad* ; Dryden read *mind* and Rowe followed. The reading is graphically easy, and attractive.

I. ii. 211. *quit the vessel, then . . .* ; F punctuates with a semi-colon after *vessel* and no stop after *me*, so that it is Ferdinand who is all afire. It is possible to justify the reading, though hardly by saying that we ' get a fine glimpse of Ferdinand hunted overboard by Ariel,' since we get that anyway. But in view of the emphasis that Ariel has been laying on the way in which he flamed all over the ship, it is I think better to assume ' transposed pointing.'

I. ii. 218. *sustaining* ; this is sometimes explained as meaning ' that helped them to float,' with a reference to Ophelia's death (*Hamlet*, IV. vii. 177-84), as though the Elizabethans held the odd belief that garments acted as life-belts. But the *Hamlet* passage does not in fact suggest anything of the kind, since it is only ' for a while ' that her clothes bear Ophelia up ; later they quite normally become ' heavy with their drink ' and pull her to muddy death. If the reading is right (it has been the object of some natural sus-picion and emendation) it must, I think, mean simply ' enduring,' *i.e.* ' undamaged.'

I. ii. 223. *sitting* ; this seems an oddly colourless and anti-climactic word after the vivid *cooling the air with sighs*. But the graphically easy *fitting* is not very appropriate to a *knot*.

I. ii. 229. *Bermoothes* ; *i.e.* the Bermudas ; a ballad on the wreck of the *Sea-Adventure* (see Preface, under ' Sources ') speaks of the *Iland of Deuils otherwise called Bermoothawes*.

I. ii. 248. *made thee no mistakings*; the New Cambridge editors, invoking compositor's hypnosis (*prithee, done thee, told thee*) omit *thee*. The metre is regularised, and the sense, I think, weakened.

I. ii. 261. *O, was she so ?*; I do not think that there need be any trouble about this phrase, still less that it is evidence of a cut. It is surely just a very characteristic expression by Prospero of a slight irritation that Ariel has got the answer to the first question of his catechism right.

I. ii. 269. *blue-eyed*; F *blew-ey'd*; the spelling *blew* is common enough, but perhaps we should read with Stanton, *blear*.

I. ii. 339. *Curs'd be I that I did so*; F reads *Curs'd be I that did so*, and almost all editors follow Steevens in regularising the metre by reading *Cursed*. But that gets the emphasis wrong on *I*, and I have ventured to regularise rather by the insertion of the second *I*.

I. ii. 342. *sty me*; F reads *Sty-me*. We are told that the hyphen is ' indicative of the force of bitterness which Caliban throws on to the first word.' Any reader who feels inclined to swallow this is invited to consider what force, of bitterness or any other emotion, Iris may be supposed to be throwing on to *turfy* in IV. i. 62, where F reads *Turphie-Mountaines*, and then to reflect whether a less imaginative explanation is not that the compositor got hold of a hyphen when he wanted a space.

I. ii. 351. *Pro. Abhorred slave . . .*; F gives this to Miranda, and the New Cambridge editors support the attribution, on the grounds that Caliban ' refers to her tuition in II. ii. 140 ' and that ' I. ii. 120 shows that she was not ignorant of life.' The pointing out of the man-in-the-moon and his dog and bush is hardly ' tuition ' of the kind that both Caliban and the speaker of this speech are referring to.   But this is a minor point; the attribution is puzzling, and I am as reluctant to desert F as the New Cambridge editors can be, but most readers will, I think, concur in feeling that it is as nearly incredible as any such thing can be that this speech (particularly in view of the two speeches which follow it) can ever have been written as Miranda's by Shakespeare.

I. ii. 377. *kiss'd The wild waves whist*; so in F, with no stop after *kiss'd*, and this is perhaps just interpretable as 'kissed the wild waves into silence,' but we should probably read a stop after *kiss'd* and take *The wild waves whist* as an 'absolute' construction—though in so enchanting a song one troubles little about grammar.

I. ii. 414. *grief (that's beauty's canker)*; the brackets are F's. The New Cambridge editors insert a stage-direction 'touching her cheek,' which, they hold, is 'supported by the significant F brackets.' And they continue, 'The faces of both lovers are tear-stained at their first meeting; Shakespeare does not do these things by accident.' The truth of this might be more acceptable if one could be sure what 'these things' are. (The brackets, which are a fact, or the stage-business, which is a conjecture?) The interpolation of this stage-direction seems to me a perfect example of the dangers of imaginative reconstruction based on inadequate data. In the first place the brackets are quite normal, as enclosing a general remark suggested by the particular instance. In the second place there is no evidence that Miranda's cheeks are tear-stained. It is true that in I. ii. 7-9, where the brackets are supposed to indicate that Miranda is fey, the New Cambridge editors also make her sob, without even the justification of brackets for their stage-direction 'sobbing'; but one interpolation is no evidence for a second. I do not for a moment wish to deny that either or both of these stage-directions *may* indicate what Shakespeare wished to happen on the stage; still less to deprecate the use of the individual imagination in the reading or the producing of Shakespeare. Every reader and every producer has to be perpetually using his wits and his imagination on the task of filling in the necessary stage-business which is needed to give colour to the dialogue and often even to make sense of it; but while he hopes that his 'business' is what Shakespeare intended, all he knows is that it is his own. And I do wish to protest against giving the apparent authority of inclusion in a rigorously authentic text to quite unauthenticated stage-directions.

I. ii. 426. *If you be maid, or no?*; Ferdinand does not so much mean 'are you a human girl rather than a goddess?' (though this may be also in his mind) as 'are you unwed?'

I. ii. 437. *and his brave son*; these words are probably the strongest evidence for the New Cambridge editors' theory of revision. Antonio's son is nowhere else mentioned in the text as we have it, and it would be a clumsy trick to mention him here merely for the sake of Prospero's reply.

I. ii. 441. *A word, good sir . . .*; why is this remark of Prospero's 'ungentle,' as Miranda calls it. Does he mean by this and by *one word more* in 448 and 451 '*only* one word more,' *i.e.* stop your talk with my daughter?

I. ii. 496. *by 's † speech*; I venture to insert *'s* in F's *by speech*.

II. i. 72. *widow Dido*; this looks as though it were some topical allusion, probably to a contemporary play, but it is unexplained. I can see no force in the attempt to connect it with Chapman's *Widow's Tears*, which has nothing to do with either Dido or Aeneas.

II. i. 82. *harp*; Amphion's, which raised the walls of Thebes.

II. i. 89. Gon. *Ay*; in F Gon. *I*. *I* is used indifferently for *Ay* or *I*, and whichever we read Gonzalo's remark is hanging in the air. Emendation is perilous, but I fancy that the New Cambridge editors are right in thinking that Gonzalo is not commenting on what has preceded but is beginning a new speech to the king, interrupted by Antonio and continued in his own next speech.

II. i. 108. *Fra.*; Except for three words at III. iii. 40 this speech is all that Francisco says in the play, though he is given three entries in stage-directions. He is therefore a somewhat mysterious figure, and may be a relic of an earlier and longer state of the play. He is particularly suspicious because this speech would be actually more appropriate to Gonzalo.

II. i. 215. *trebles*; F *trebbles*. Rowe read *troubles*, and the New Cambridge editors approve, on the grounds that (*a*) if the compositor had *troubles* in front of him he had only to make the common *e:o* error and mistake a *v* for a *b* to get *trebbles*, and that (*b*) 'the next line—"standing water"—requires "troubles," *cf. The Taming of the Shrew*, V. ii. 142; "A woman moved is like a fountain troubled."' But (*a*) why should the compositor, with a perfectly ordinary word in front of him, go out of his way to misread *o* as *e* (admittedly easy enough) and *v* or *u* as *b* (not at all so easy) to produce a less natural word? and (*b*) what in the world has the line from *The Taming of the Shrew* got to do with it? The fact that Shakespeare elsewhere uses the not uncommon word 'troubles' in connection with water is no sort of proof that he is doing so here. Sebastian need not be saying more than 'this sounds interesting; I will be quiet and heed you.' *Trebles thee o'er* is certainly an odd phrase for 'makes you three times the person you are,' but not any odder than 'trouble o'er' in the sense of 'o'er-trouble,' *i.e.* 'give too much trouble to'; and he will be 'trebled,' I think, because he will displace the King, Ferdinand, and Claribel.

II. i. 237. *But doubt discovery there*; in spite of attempts to explain this it seems to me to mean nothing; the New Cambridge editors follow Nicholson and read *douts* for *doubt*, with the interpretation ' even Ambition cannot look beyond a crown, but there puts out her torch of discovery.' This at least means something.

II. ii. 27. *a kind of, not of the newest Poor-John*; the comma is F's. The New Cambridge editors omit it, apparently without a thought, and certainly without a comment. This is unexpected, since to the devotee of F's punctuation it is surely a gem of purest ray, an ' exquisite ' comma. It expresses the hesitation of Trinculo while he casts about for the right description of the smell. To the faithless it is of course merely a blunder.

II. ii. 84. *to you, cat*; referring certainly to the proverb that liquor will make a cat talk; but I cannot help feeling that *to your cat* (*i.e.* the cat i' the adage) would run more easily than the abrupt vocative.

II. ii. 99. *I have no long spoon*; ' he that sups with the devil must have a long spoon.'

II. ii. 171. *scamels*; this appears to be a *vox nihili*. For various reasons, partly sense and partly the probable source in Strachey, there seems to me little doubt that *sea-mells* (*i.e.* sea-mews, of which the young were a delicacy) is the right reading.

II. ii. 175. *fellow Trinculo*; should one perhaps read *follow, Trinculo*?

II. ii. 182. *trencher*; F reads *trenchering*, which the New Cambridge editors defend on the ground that Caliban is drunk. Between the drunkenness of Caliban and a possible hypnotic trance of the compositor, induced by *firing* and *requiring*, there seems to me little to choose.

III. i. 15. *Most busy lest, when I do it*; I shall add nothing to the mountain of conjectural emendation that has been heaped on this unhappy half line. I will only suggest that if *easilest* is a possible Shakespearean or compositorial spelling of *easiliest* (see *Cymbeline*, IV. ii. 207), so is *busilest* or *busylest* of *busiliest*, and that Ferdinand may mean ' I am at the moment being neglectful, but these sweet thoughts refresh me even when I am pursuing my labours most busily.' For this interpretation Theobald's reading of *labour* for *labours* would simplify things. This has perhaps the advantage that it gives some force to the adversative *but*, and to the *even*. The trouble is, of course, the comma.

III. i. 33. *'tis fresh morning* . . .; ' This is curious, as the lovers had never been in each other's company at night. Possibly a relic of the earlier version' (New Cambridge). A remarkable note, and an example of the *idée fixe*; it will be observed that by this stage of the play we are supposed to have accepted ' the' earlier version as an established fact. Does Ferdinand, in fact, mean any more than ' when you are here I should be as fresh as a daisy even after a day's work,' *i.e.* by night qualifies *fresh morning* rather than *when you are by*, which might be better bracketed.

III. ii. 4. *the folly of this island !*; the New Cambridge editors characterise this phrase as pointless. They say that Trinculo toasts Stephano (inserting an unauthenticated stage-direction to that effect) as *the Sophy of this island !* But why, in the name of common sense, should the drunken Trinculo mean anything more than ' how this island turns our brains ! '?

III. ii. 121. *scout*; the New Cambridge editors are perhaps right in retaining F's *cout* for the first occurrence. *Cout* is a variant of ' colt,' *i.e.* ' make a fool of,' and the second time F reads *skowt*.

III. iii. 45. *dew-lapp'd* . . .; *i.e.* with the goitre common to mountain-dwellers.

III. iii. 84. *devouring*; the New Cambridge editors suggest that

this perhaps should be 'devoiring,' *i.e.* 'waiting at table.' Seeing
that all the waiting at table that Ariel has done is to cause the removal
of the banquet before anyone has tasted it, comment seems to be
needless.

III. iii. 106. *the spirits*; why should it be 'compositor's grammar'
(New Cambridge) to read a natural plural? There is more to be
said for reading *their*.

IV. i. 3. *third*; commonly emended to *thrid*; but the New Cambridge editors are surely right in defending F. The thirds are Prospero, his dead wife, and Miranda.

IV. i. 9. *her off*; F *her of*. Perhaps *hereof* (New Cambridge).

IV. i. 64. *pioned and twilled*; a mere list of emendations will illustrate
the trouble that there has been about this phrase; for *pioned* we
have *pionied, peonied, peoned, pansies pied*, and, for *twilled, tulip'd, tilled,
lilied, willow'd* and *twisted*. On this mass of conjecture I will only add
that what may be called the 'flowery' conjectures seem to me to
be on the wrong lines, since as the picture is developed we seem
to have first the banks, then their brims (however described) and
then the betrimming of them with flowers for the cold nymphs'
crowns, whereas if the banks are first described as adorned with
specific flowers the following line is something of an anticlimax.
For the 'agricultural' interpretation, which is, I think, the least
unsatisfactory, see the Glossary.

IV. i. 89. *dusky Dis . ..* ; Pluto or Dis, the god of the underworld,
carried off Ceres' daughter Proserpine.

IV. i. 110. *Earth's*; perhaps *Earthës* (Aldis Wright).

IV. i. 123. *So rare a wonder'd father . . .*; surely a very odd remark.
It is not natural for the enthusiastic young lovers to say that his
father-in-law to be, however rich in wonders, makes any place
Paradise. Some copies of F read *wife* for *wise*, which would help

things. And the attribution of *Sweet, now, silence* to Prospero is a trifle suspicious. If it is right he must be addressing Miranda, who has said nothing. But the attribution to Miranda does not really solve the trouble, since it will not work with *our spell*.

IV. i. 146. *You do look, my son . . .*; the critics who would allot the masque to another hand regard this and the next line as a clumsy link with the re-beginning of Shakespeare at *Our revels*. The metre no doubt is somewhat harsh. But I am not clear that there is much in the argument that it is Prospero, not Ferdinand, who looks dismayed and needs to be told to be cheerful. But there is something in it, and if we are to embark on conjecture I should guess that what happened, at some stage of transmission, was something like the famous 'proud Scot' passage in 1 *Henry IV*, V. iii. 11. *I.e.* that these lines originally belonged to Miranda, continuing her speech, and reading

> *You look, my father, in a moved sort*

and that Prospero did not begin till *Our revels*; that then the speech-heading for Prospero got displaced two lines too high, and that to regularise the sense someone emended *father* to *son* and inserted *do* for the syllabic count. One can catch the Folio elsewhere scanning by syllables and not by ear.

IV. i. 154. *all which it inherit*; it seems almost sacrilegious to write a note on so famous a passage; but I suspect that I am not alone in having always unthinkingly taken these words in a sense which is at best dubious, namely, 'all which it possesses'; I still believe that that is what Shakespeare meant, whether or not he wrote an *s* which was omitted before the initial *s* of *shall*; but there is no doubt that as they stand the words mean 'all things that possess it.'

IV. i. 164. *I thank thee, Ariel*; the New Cambridge editors boldly read *I think thee*. The emendation is brilliant, and graphically easy;

the resultant reading is, I think, hopelessly un-Shakespearean. Ariel is too concrete a figure to be 'thought' into existence or presence. But I am sure, too, that the New Cambridge editors are right in feeling that the line as it stands is suspect.

IV. i. 184. *O'er-stunk their feet*; I do not think that there is any need for complicated emendations of *feet* to *sweat*, with the comment 'their feet, being at the bottom of the pool, could hardly be offensive.' For the matter of that, all of them was in the pool except their faces. I do not think that there is more to it than a compression; their feet are well submerged by the pool, which, anyway, is so foul that it is more unsavoury than their feet even if unsubmerged.

IV. i. 231. *Let's alone*; if we are to emend, I would much prefer the *let 't alone* of Rowe (see l. 223) to either *let's along* or *let's all on*.

IV. i. 235. *Mistress line . . .*; it is important in the first place to realise that Stephano is addressing a lime tree and not a clothes-line; see l. 193 above, and the *line-grove* of V. i. 10. In the second place, none of the explanations of the line-baldness joke which follows carry much conviction. I suspect that (Stephano being Stephano) they are all too delicate.

IV. i. 239. *Do, do*; apparently pointless. The New Cambridge editors make the most attractive suggestion *Do-de* (see *King Lear*, III. iv. 57, in F).

V. i. 60. (*Now useless*) *boil*; I retain F's punctuation, since I think it is just explicable as a harsh instance of the omitted relative, *i.e.* 'thy brains which are seething.' The reading of *the* for *thy* would make this easier. The usual reading is *boil'd*, but the New Cambridge editors read *Now useless boil*, *i.e.* 'your brain is merely a tumour'; but the omission of *a* seems as harsh as that of *which*.

V. i. 61. The New Cambridge editors adduce a number of earlier broken lines as evidence of revision or cutting; here they comment, 'This broken line is too effective not to be intentional.' Is the cake eaten or had?

V. i. 145. *and supportable . . .*; the New Cambridge editors comment as follows:—'Capell jestingly remarks that *supportable* is insupportable. Perhaps the solution is to divide that word, retain the F *deere* for *dear*, and read *less* for *loss* (an *e:o* misprint, induced by the hypnotic influence of *loss* thrice repeated in the preceding lines). *Dere* or *deere*=pain, injury, *v*. O.E.D., which quotes Chaucer, Malory, Chapman, etc. This would give us:

> *As great to me as late, and support, able*
> *To make the dere less, have I means . . .*

i.e. Prospero says in effect: "I have means of support weaker than yours to comfort my sad heart; for I have lost my daughter—the only woman left to me."' But all the pother seems hardly worth while, since Prospero says exactly the same 'in effect' with the text as it stands, and the only real awkwardness, 'in effect' with the text first syllable of *supportable*, is left just where it was. (There is no awkwardness in the accent on *-able*, since this suffix is frequently, in Shakespeare, to be pronounced just like the plain adjective.)

V. i. 174. *Yes, for a score*; the emendation *Yet* for *Yes* is commended as 'self-evident.' But is it even plausible? Miranda's *Yes* picks up Ferdinand's *No* two lines above, as the *score of kingdoms* picks up *the world*.

Wrangle, however slight the support of dictionaries, must, I think, in the context mean 'play false.' And we should perhaps compare the very awkward *wrong led* in *Antony and Cleopatra*, III. vi. 80, where *wrangled* (in the above sense) would solve difficulties both of rhythm and meaning.

Glossary

MANY words and phrases in Shakespeare require glossing, not because they are in themselves unfamiliar, but for the opposite reason, that Shakespeare uses in their Elizabethan and unfamiliar sense a large number of words which seem so familiar that there is no incentive to look for them in the glossary. It is hoped that a glossary arranged as below will make it easy to see at a glance what words and phrases in any particular scene require elucidation. A number of phrases are glossed by what seems to be, in their context, the modern equivalent rather than by lexicographical glosses on the words which compose them.

Act First

SCENE I

line

3 YARELY, smartly
23 HAND, handle
29 COMPLEXION, face

line

32 ADVANTAGE, help
55 WIDE-CHOPP'D, wide-mouthed

SCENE II

4 WELKIN, sky
13 FRAUGHTING, forming the freight
29 SOIL, damage
35 BOOTLESS, profitless
41 OUT, fully
53 SINCE, ago
64 TEEN, trouble
65 FROM, outside
70 MANAGE, management

71 THROUGH, among
SIGNORIES, 'N. Italian states governed by princes'
72 PRIME, leading
81 TRASH, slow down a hound by hanging weight on neck
OVER-TOPPING, outstripping the rest
90 CLOSENESS, being a recluse

Act I Sc. ii—*continued*

line
92 O'ER-PRIZ'D, surpassed in value
97 BEING . . . LORDED, having gained control
112 DRY, thirsty
123 PREMISES, stipulated terms
125 PRESENTLY, at once
134 HINT, 'cue'
138 IMPERTINENT, irrelevant
144 IN FEW, in short
146 CARCASS OF A BUTT, 'tub of a barrel'
157 UNDERGOING STOMACH, temper of endurance
165 STEADED, helped
194 TO POINT, precisely, 'just so'
200 DISTINCTLY, separately
207 COIL, ado
213 UP-STARING, standing on end (*cf. modern use of an animal's coat 'staring'*)
218 SUSTAINING, surviving

line
234 FLOTE, sea
240 GLASSES, hours
295 HIS, its
311 MISS, do without
317 QUAINT, 'cute'
326 URCHINS, hedgehogs
370 ACHES, a disyllable
379 FEATLY, neatly
380 BURTHEN, chorus
404 REMEMBER, recall
406 OWES, owns
413 BUT, except that
417 NATURAL, mortal
424 PRIME, main
431 SINGLE, poor (*from sense of 'lonely'*)
450 UNEASY, difficult
453 OW'ST, ownest
467 FEARFUL, coward
470 FROM THY WARD, drop your guard

Act Second

SCENE I

3 HINT, occasion, prompting
18 DOLLAR, *orig. the German thaler*
95 BATE, 'shut up'
104 RATE, reckoning
128 MO, more (*Eliz. plur.*)
137 CLOUDY, sullen

147 BOURN, boundary
156 ENGINE, mechanism
158 FOISON, plenty
168 SENSIBLE, sensitive
242 NOTE, news
POST, messenger

line		line	
260	CHOUGH, jackdaw	273	CANDIED, frozen
267	FEATER, more smartly	279	WINK, sleep
270	KIBE, ulcerated chilblain	283	TELL THE CLOCK, mark the time
271	PUT ME TO, make me wear	315	VERILY, the truth

SCENE II

3	BY INCH-MEAL, inch by inch (*cf.* '*piecemeal*')	39	GABERDINE, coat, cloak
5	URCHIN-SHOWS, goblin-shows (*the hedgehog being the traditional embodiment of the devil*)	46	SWABBER, deck-scrubber
		71	NEAT'S-LEATHER, cowhide
		87	CHAPS, jaws
9	MOW, grimace	106	SIEGE, excrement, 'stool'
21	BOMBARD, large leather vessel	121	BUTT, barrel
		146	DRAWN, drunk

Act Third

SCENE I

2	SETS OFF, counterbalances	57	LIKE OF, be fond of
50	GLASS, mirror	79	WANT, lack

SCENE II

9	SET, with fixed stare	63	PIED, motley
12	SACK, wine of sherry character		PATCH, clown
16	STANDARD, standard-bearer (*with pun in next line in sense of one who can stand up*)	67	QUICK FRESHES, fresh springs
		70	STOCK-FISH, salt-fish
		80	MURRAIN, (cattle-) plague
17	LIST, like	91	WEZAND, gullet
19	GO, walk	118	WHILE-ERE, a while ago
32	NATURAL, idiot	151	TABORER, player of small drum
59	PARTY, person concerned		

SCENE III

line

1 BY'R LAKIN, by our lady-kin
5 ATTACH'D WITH, arrested by
21 DROLLERY, puppet-show
32 GENTLE, *in the 'gentle'man sense*
48 PUTTER-OUT OF FIVE FOR ONE, gambling insurer against risks of travel
54 TO, as its

line

60 PROPER, own
65 DOWLE, feather
66 LIKE, also
85 BATED, scented
99 BASS, give the ground-bass to
102 BUT ONE FIEND AT A TIME, so long as there is only one fiend at once

Act Fourth

SCENE I

7 STRANGELY, rarely
16 SANCTIMONIOUS, holy
18 ASPERSION, sprinkling (holy water)
42 PRESENTLY, at once
47 MOP AND MOW, grimaces
50 CONCEIVE, understand
57 COROLLARY, overplus
63 STOVER, grass for hay
64 PIONED, (?) dug deep
TWILLED, (?) ridged
68 POLE-CLIPT, in which poles are embraced by vines; *or*, enclosed by poles
81 BOSKY, shadowy

82 SCARF, adornment
89 THAT, by which
90 SCANDAL'D, scandalous
98 MINION, darling
110 FOISON, abundance
130 CRISP, rippled
143 PASSION, emotion
175 TABOR, small drum
180 GOSS, gorse
187 STALE, bait
193 LINE, lime-tree
236 JERKIN, jacket
261 PARD, leopard
CAT O' MOUNTAIN, wild-cat

Act Fifth

SCENE I

line

4 SIXTH HOUR, six o'clock
10 LINE-GROVE, lime-grove
11 YOUR RELEASE, you release them
17 EAVES OF REEDS, *i.e.* thatched roofs
24 PASSION, feel
47 SPURS, roots
64 FALL, let fall
81 REASONABLE SHORE, shore of reason

line

101 PRESENTLY, immediately
223 GLASSES, hours
234 MO, more (*Eliz. plur.*)
240 MOPING, bemused
247 INFEST, trouble
248 PICK'D LEISURE, appointed time of leisure
249 SINGLE, complete
250 EVERY, every one of

Epilogue

13 WANT, lack